The Authentic Edge: Leading Without Losing Yourself

A Leadership Guide for Black Men Moving from Middle Management to the Executive Table

Dominic George

Vision Leadership for LIFE

Publisher: Vision Leadership for LIFE - LLC
Email: admin@visionleadershipforlife.com
Website: www.visionleadershipforlife.com
LinkedIn: www.linkedin.com/in/dominiccgeorge
July 2025

FOREWARD

In *The Authentic Edge: Leading Without Losing Yourself*, Dominic George creates a dialogue with his reader that speaks to the lived experiences of Black men in leadership. He lends a voice to tethered individuals who have been visible yet unseen, and who are burdened with the pressures of representing their identity not as a leader, but as a "Black leader". This work acts as a mirror, one of those rarities that reads YOU, naming truths that you've only whispered to yourself in moments of solitude and deep reflection.

Sectioned into four parts, *The Authentic Edge* provides a roadmap to success, deeply rooted in the experiences of its author. Dominic walks us through the various phases of his climb through executive leadership and becomes a metaphor for bridging the gap between aspiration and achievement. This literary framework for Black leaders is not solely a guidebook, but a call to action, a challenge, a strategy, and a reclamation of one's inner strength and identity.

The complexities of identity are central to the overall theme of this work, the idea of staying whole while leading is a tug-of-war that many of us face as we transcend to heights unknown. Identity is often lost in Black men in the workplace as this concept of code-switching becomes a survival tactic and a necessity for success. Black men are often forced to surrender their presence for palatability, and experience the constant rigmarole of staying two steps ahead just to be "seen" as qualified, a familiar crossroads that I have endured. Recognizing this plight, Dominic provides a simple, yet effective solution; use your authenticity as a strategy instead of as a liability. *The Authentic Edge* does something unique here: it grants us permission to be aligned, transparent, value-driven and human.

It is the aforementioned that moved me most as I continued to turn the pages of this book. There was a rhythm that was being created for me of self-examination and empowerment. There were previous elements of my life that I never self-reflected on, as well as experiences and traumas that I never acknowledged that molded me into the leader and entrepreneur I am today. Dominic, through his work, created a testimony for me that I could not verbalize and actualize for myself not because of my inability to be introspective, but simply because no one had ever asked me to hold a mirror to myself and reflect on my *"why's", "what's", "where's" and "how's"*. I had silently and begrudgingly completed the work over the years to repair and elevate myself; however, I was unaware of the weight of the experiences that caused me to do so.

The Authentic Edge creates a spectrum of resonance; it is not a common occurrence to find a guidebook that is "for us, by us". Dominic's voice is one that has been tempered by experience and sharpened with purpose, inciting a point of view that critiques the reader in a way that empowers and catapults Black men to be the best, most authentic version of themselves. The most poignant insight that Dominic provided me wasn't about my ability to overcome obstacles and ascend to higher roles within a structured corporate regime that was not made for me, but how I aligned myself to be unapologetically me. I am a Black man worthy of all my achievements, my status as an impactful leader, and a champion of my own self-definition. It is a beautiful, thoughtful and intentional work of art that transforms us from subjugation to triumph.

The ability to bring a reader to such a pivotal "aha moment" comes as no surprise. Dominic, in his professional and personal life, is a coach, a speaker and a mentor. He does not just talk about leadership, he multiplies it. He creates pathways for Black men across varying industries to find their voice, strengthen their presence and elevate their impact, while staying authentic to oneself and not diluting their truths. Dominic has not only created a path to professional development, but also a key to personal liberation. He is teaching us how to navigate a system that was not designed for us, and he instills in us that the crucial elements of freedom and true self-identity are the necessary catalyst to successfully lead and create a lasting impact for self and for the generations of Black male leaders to come.

To Dominic: Thank you for providing a voice and space that depicts what so many of us have lived, and for writing this with such grace, compassion, intelligence and urgency. Your voice and insight are not just necessary, they are catalytic and monumental.

To the reader: It is no accident that *The Authentic Edge* is in your hands. You are reading this because something in you is ready for change, ready to break free from performance and shrinking, and ready to step into a space of leading with truth.

In these pages, I pray that you find the permission you didn't know you needed, the tools you've been missing, and the reflection of the leader you have always been destined to become.

Larry Buckhannon,

Leader of Leaders, Multinational Supermarket Chain and Chief Executive Officer, Buckhannon Consultancy Group

TABLE OF CONTENTS

INTRODUCTION:

THE COST OF PLAYING THE GAME

The hardest part of my leadership journey as a Black man rising through the executive ranks wasn't the workload or the pressure, it was learning how to lead while being constantly surveilled.

Not just watched, but interpreted. Every word, every expression, every decision was filtered through someone else's lens of who they believed I should be.

I remember sitting at a conference table in a director's role, the only Black man in the room. I presented strategic ideas, data-backed and forward-thinking, but they were either redirected or dismissed. Then, twenty minutes later, those same ideas would be reintroduced by someone else, typically a white peer, and suddenly they were seen as brilliant.

That's when I realized I wasn't just leading, I was translating.

Constantly adjusting my tone, my posture, my presence, not to be effective, but to be accepted.

That's what made the journey heavy for me. Not the complexity of the work, but the emotional calluses formed behind every interaction.

I constantly questioned myself: Do I speak up now, or will I be seen as aggressive? Do I advocate for my team, or will I be viewed as too invested?

The real danger wasn't burnout. It was erasure, slowly losing the very essence of what made me an effective leader in the first place. That's the cost of playing the game. I had to decide: either keep contorting myself to fit someone else's mold, or lead from a place of unapologetic alignment.

When I chose the latter, everything shifted. That's when the executive table became mine to own, not just mine to earn.

The Daily Negotiation

Balancing corporate expectations with my authenticity wasn't really a balance at all, it was a daily negotiation. And truthfully, for a long time, I was losing that negotiation.

During my tenure as a senior manager, I inherited a team that was underperforming. Morale was low, trust was fragile, and they were accustomed to being micromanaged. My authentic leadership style was grounded in transparency, building relational equity, and challenging people to rise, not retreat. But the message from above was clear: drive results quickly and don't get distracted by the "people side."

That was my crossroads. Do I meet their expectations and become the kind of leader they're comfortable with, cold, performance-obsessed, and disconnected? Or do I trust the approach rooted in who I am, transformative, people-centered, demanding yet affirming?

I decided I wasn't going to strip myself down to fit someone else's definition of executive readiness. Instead, I began having what I call "quiet power conversations", addressing the elephant in the room with grace, not guilt. I modeled transparency with my team, even when leadership didn't. And when results followed, I made sure people knew how we got there: through trust, not tyranny.

That's the balance, not pretending there's no game, but refusing to lose your soul trying to win it. I learned how to play the game without becoming it. When you start leading from that place where your strategy and your spirit are aligned, it's not just balance, it's power.

The Luxury of Authenticity

I believe authenticity often feels like a luxury in leadership, especially for many of us as Black men, because it was rarely presented to us as a viable path to power. Instead, we were taught to suppress it, manage it, or market it, but not to fully embrace it.

I'll never forget being coached by a senior executive early in my director role. He said, *"You're good, but if you want to make that vice president track, you've got to soften your presence, be less intense."*

I wasn't yelling or being disrespectful. I was direct, prepared, and passionate about results. But in that space, my confidence was misread as aggression.

That moment stuck with me, not because it broke me, but because it reminded me: the closer we get to power, the more we're expected to dilute what got us there in the first place. That's why authenticity feels like a luxury. It's not always safe, and it's certainly not always rewarded. Let's be real, we've all seen it.

The brother who speaks truth in the wrong meeting and disappears from the next org chart. The leader who challenges bias during performance reviews and suddenly gets labeled "hard to work with." So, we adjust. We shrink.

We contort ourselves into polished, palatable versions of leadership that check all the boxes, but leave us exhausted.

But here's the shift: when I stopped seeing authenticity as a threat and started treating it as a strategy, everything changed. I began choosing alignment over assimilation.

I started naming my values up front in interviews, leading with clarity in difficult conversations, and showing up consistently, not just when it felt safe. That built trust. That built influence. Authenticity isn't soft. It's surgical.

But to use it well, you have to stop waiting for permission, and start treating your truth as a leadership asset, not a liability.

Clarity, Not Control

There was a point in my leadership journey when I mistook aggression for strength. I didn't call it that at the time. I called it drive. I called it excellence. But underneath it all was something else: the pressure to prove myself, to over-deliver, to be undeniable, to never give anyone a reason to question whether I belonged in the room. It wasn't ignorance. It was armor. And for a while, it worked, until it didn't.

The turning point came during a high-stakes project where I was tasked with leading cross-functional teams through a strategic overhaul. I came in with clarity, vision, and urgency. I knew what needed to happen, and I pushed hard, on timelines, on people, on process.

I was forceful, not because I craved power, but because I didn't trust the space to respect me without it. And I think that's what happens when you've been overlooked too many times: you start to lead with your fists instead of your feet.

We got results, but at a cost. Morale was low. Collaboration was shallow. I had the respect of the C-suite, but not the trust of my team. They delivered because they had to, not because they wanted to.

And deep down, I knew: I wasn't proud of how I led. That was the hard truth. I was winning battles, but I was losing people. And worse, I was losing myself.

I realized that aggression wasn't giving me an edge. It was masking my fear. Fear that if I didn't lead hard, I wouldn't be taken seriously. But leadership rooted in fear can't sustain you. It fractures you. It breeds the very burnout, isolation, and resentment you're trying to avoid. That's when I started to shift.

I began practicing alignment, leading from clarity, not control. Centering my values, not just my goals. Owning the room with presence, not pressure.

It changed everything. The more I led with alignment, the more influence I gained, not just authority. Teams began to trust me, not merely comply with me. I didn't have to yell to be heard. I didn't have to bulldoze to be respected. Because the truth is: real leadership power doesn't come from proving people wrong. It comes from standing firmly in what's right for you. Aggression may get you attention, but alignment earns trust, and trust is the currency of true leadership.

The impact of authentic leadership is profound. It's leadership, not just performance. Authentic leadership isn't about feeling good; it's about doing good in a way that doesn't cost you your peace, your purpose, or your people.

For individuals, especially Black men in leadership, authenticity is oxygen. It's the antidote to burnout, impostor syndrome, and the chronic code-switching that drains us. When a Black man leads from his authentic self, he stops performing and starts transforming. He walks into rooms knowing he belongs, not because he's perfect, but because he's prepared. His decisions come from values, not fear. His leadership carries weight, not just value.

For organizations, authentic leadership is the difference between compliance and culture. When leaders show up whole, they give their teams permission to do the same. It builds psychological safety. It creates environments where innovation isn't punished and truth isn't a liability. It sets the tone for trust, and trust is what turns average teams into high-performing ones.

Let's be clear: this kind of leadership isn't always comfortable. It will challenge norms. It will disrupt systems. But that's exactly the point. When Black men lead from alignment, not aggression or assimilation, we don't just shift boardrooms; we shift paradigms. We model a new way to succeed without losing ourselves. We raise the standard, not by becoming more like them, but by becoming more of who we already are.

That's the legacy of authentic leadership. It doesn't just change your title, it changes the entire table.

I didn't write this book to impress anyone. I wrote it because I know what it feels like to lead on paper and feel lost behind the scenes. I know the pressure of performing excellence while quietly wondering if I'm still myself. I know the weight of being the only one, while trying not to be the wrong one. I know what it's like to be celebrated for your output and yet feel invisible in your full identity.

And I know I'm not the only one. Too many Black men are leading in rooms that applaud their results but erase their reality. We're strategizing, building, succeeding, but doing it all while edited, quieted, exhausted, and alone.

I'm writing this book because I refuse to let authenticity be a luxury Black men in leadership can't afford. I'm writing for those who are done performing strength and ready to lead with soul. For those who want to rise, but not at the cost of their rhythm, their voice, their peace. For those who know they were made for more but are tired of shape-shifting just to stay at the table.

This book is a strategy. A reflection. A reclaiming. You won't find leadership clichés here, you'll find lived wisdom, hard-won clarity, and a pathway back to yourself. Because leadership should never cost you your identity.

It's time to cut the cord. Your edge is the authentic one. You were always built to lead from it. That's why I wrote this book: to mark a beginning.

PART 1:

THE IDENTITY CRISIS OF LEADERSHIP

Chapter 1:

You're Not Crazy It Is That Hard

The micro-tensions of leadership as a Black man don't appear in your job description, but they shape every room you enter. They're the signals, the coded corrections, the quiet recalibrations you make to appear competent but not threatening, assertive but not angry, passionate but not emotional. I felt these tensions in a thousand subtle ways. They never showed up in performance reviews, but they absolutely affected both my performance and my peace.

There was a time I presented a bold, well-researched idea during a strategy meeting, only for it to be ignored, then repeated by a colleague minutes later and praised. I remember how quickly feedback on my tone would come whenever I asked direct questions or challenged assumptions with data. I've seen the discomfort in stakeholder spaces the moment I entered the room, confident and prepared, before I even said a word.

The Weight of Micro-Tensions

These moments don't come with sirens. They come with silence, and they add up. Over time, you begin to self-edit. You start second-guessing. You practice what I call emotional triage: managing other people's perceptions while suppressing your own instincts. The psychological weight is exhausting, not because we're incapable, but because we're carrying more than most people will ever have to see.

These micro-tensions didn't stop my career, but they slowed my trust in myself. They made me over-prepare, over-deliver, and under-express. Over time, they almost made me forget how powerful my unfiltered voice really was. That's why I say: you're not crazy, it really is that hard. Not because we're weak, but because we've been carrying the weight that leadership culture refuses to acknowledge.

I remember what Malik, a regional director in healthcare operations, said to me during a coaching session:

"What wears you down isn't the job. It's the second job of always having to prove, explain, or defend your presence. Most of us aren't tired from the work, we're tired from constantly managing other people's discomfort with our leadership."

The pressure to fit in doesn't just impact your behavior, it starts to chip away at your identity. In the workplace, especially in leadership, fitting in becomes a performance: a performance of neutrality, of politeness over presence, of strategic silence over inconvenient truth.

For Black men, that performance isn't optional. It's often the unspoken requirement for simply surviving in the space.

When Fitting In Becomes a Mask

I remember being in a high-visibility leadership program, a hand-picked position labeled as "one to watch." But behind the curtain, I was constantly adjusting. I smiled more than I wanted to. I avoided cultural references that felt "too Black." I measured the tone of my emails like I was drafting legal copy.

Eventually, I realized I was being praised for a version of myself that wasn't really me. I was fitting in, but I wasn't belonging.

That's where the damage begins. Because when you keep shape-shifting to stay safe, you eventually lose clarity about who you are. You start doubting your instincts. You question your voice. You wonder, Is it safe to be me here? The more you ask that question, the more your authenticity begins to feel like a liability, not a leadership edge.

Here's what I've learned the hard way: Fitting in is camouflage; belonging is clarity.

The moment you start leading from who you really are, not from who you think they need you to be, is the moment you begin to reclaim your power. It's risky, yes. But it's also real.

Realness builds trust. It builds culture. And most of all, it builds the kind of leadership that doesn't crumble under pressure, because it was never built on pretense.

Tariq, a VP of People and Culture at a national nonprofit, once said during one of our sessions after completing an exercise:

"I stopped trying to mimic executive presence and started defining my own. Where I'm from and how I see the world isn't a weakness, it's a lens that makes my leadership necessary. Once I owned that, everything aligned."

That's the goal: to move toward alignment with who you truly are.

When you're fitting in, you're not being seen, you're being scanned. You become fluent in the politics of presence. You start asking three specific questions:

- How should I say this so they don't read it the wrong way?
- Should I speak now, or will I be seen as aggressive?
- Can I push back without becoming the problem?

That's camouflage, a survival strategy, not a leadership stance.

What I've learned is that camouflage teaches you how to blend, not how to lead. You adapt your language, your posture, even your vision to match what feels palatable in the room. But the more you camouflage, the more distant you become from your own leadership instincts. You don't lose your voice, you lose your sense of self, because you're constantly reacting instead of leading with intention.

Now contrast that with belonging. Belonging isn't about changing yourself to be accepted; it's about being so clear on who you are that the room adjusts to you. Belonging is clarity. It's when your values, your leadership style, and your story align, and you don't apologize for it. It's knowing, "I have a voice here, and I don't need to shrink it." It's knowing my perspective isn't extra, it's essential. It's understanding that I don't just have a seat at the table; I know exactly why I'm sitting there.

Here's the truth most systems don't tell you: you can't camouflage your way into clarity. You have to make a decision: Do you want to blend in, or do you want to belong? Belonging takes more risks. It comes with tension, but it also comes with power, the kind that doesn't evaporate when the environment shifts. The kind that isn't dependent on approval, but rooted in alignment.

Because the moment you stop leading to survive and start leading to stand, that's when everything changes. Not just for you, but for everyone watching. You prove that authenticity is strategy, not softness.

There was a season in my career when the mask didn't just make appearances, it became my leadership identity. I had been promoted to a high-profile role, reporting directly to senior executives, essentially the senior leadership team, known for being politically sharp but culturally tone-deaf. The pressure was immediate. I was now responsible for delivering big wins on tight timelines, under intense scrutiny, with no room for error. Unspoken but clearly understood, I knew I was being watched, not just as a leader, but as a Black leader.

So I put on the mask. I softened my language in meetings. I offered filtered feedback in one-on-ones, even when it cost my team. I avoided direct challenges, even when I disagreed with strategy. I dressed the part. Spoke the part. I even started adopting language that made me feel like I was reading from a script instead of speaking from my soul.

And the mask worked. I was praised for my professionalism, for staying calm under pressure, for fitting in well with senior leadership. But what they were really saying was, "Thank you for being non-threatening." What they didn't see was that I was dying inside. I was succeeding, but I was disconnected, from my team, from my values, and from the very fire that made me a leader in the first place. Every meeting became a performance. Every email, a rehearsal. And eventually, the mask grew too heavy.

The breaking point came during a project debrief, when a senior leader blatantly took credit for a decision I had made, one that had saved the entire initiative from failure. I had the receipts. I had my team's respect. But I said nothing. Because the mask told me,

"Don't rock the boat. Play the long game. Be patient."

That's when I realized: I wasn't leading. I was just surviving.

So I made a shift, slowly but intentionally. I began to speak up, not recklessly, but unapologetically. I started mentoring other leaders from a place of honesty, not perfection. I stopped mirroring what was comfortable and started embodying what was rooted in conviction.

And yes, some people pulled back, but the right ones leaned into the process.

Most importantly, I got my voice back.

Because the truth is: the mask may get you in the room, but it will never help you own the room. And if success costs you your authenticity, it's not success, it's silent suffering with a six-figure title.

Andre, a chief legal officer at a Fortune 500 fintech company I was coaching, said during one of our calls:

"Being the only one in the room isn't just lonely, it's political. You're not just carrying your voice; you're carrying perception. I had to learn how to lead with quiet power, how to show up without shrinking and influence without performing."

It's a risk, but in essence, you have to learn how to take the risk of being authentic with yourself.

You know you're wearing a mask when you look in the mirror and realize you're no longer yourself, when you start acting one way in one space and a different way in another.

There's always room to evolve past the mask. Always room to let it go.

It's about surrounding yourself with people you trust, people who will tell you the truth. It's about building community, being in reflection with others who affirm who you are.

So when you walk into spaces where you may be the only one, or where you feel like you can't fully be yourself, those people remind you there's a different version of you, one that's real and whole.

The hardest part of leadership isn't the pressure. It's the split between the mirror and the mask, the internal conflict between who I am when no one's watching, and who I've been conditioned to become when I walk into the room.

Behind closed doors, I know exactly who I am. I'm grounded, clear, and honest. I don't need to prove anything. I lead with instinct, integrity, and vision. That's the mirror, the version of me that doesn't perform; it simply exists.

But the moment I step into certain rooms, I feel the shift. My posture tightens, my language adjusts, and my emotional range narrows. I'm no longer just thinking about the work; I'm calculating how my presence will be perceived. That's the mask.

For years, I lived in that conflict. The mirror reminded me of my values, what I stood for and what I believed. But the mask reminded me of the stakes: how quickly perception can turn, how fragile respect can be when you're the only one in the room who looks like you.

The tension is real. I would ask myself: Am I being strategic, or am I shrinking? Am I adapting, or am I erasing? Am I protecting my career, or am I betraying my calling?

Over time, I've learned how to navigate that tension. I don't pretend it isn't there, I honor it. Because that tension is not a weakness; it's a signal. It means I'm still in touch with myself. It means I haven't gone numb to the difference between performance and presence.

More importantly, I treat alignment as a discipline. Before I enter any room, I ask myself: What does leadership look like for me, on my terms? What do I need to protect my voice? Where can I hold the line without losing the moment?

This internal work keeps me grounded. It reminds me that who I am when no one's watching isn't a liability, it's my leadership blueprint. The more I align with that version of myself, the less I need the mask. The less I lead from fear, the more I lead with authority, not just the authority that comes with a title, but authority rooted in my truth.

Because what I've learned is this: if the role you're playing in the room keeps you disconnected from the man you see in the mirror, it's time to rewrite the script.

I'm reminded of Evan, a former COO and executive coach in the education sector, who once told me, "I didn't burn out from working hard. I burned out from working disconnected from my values, my voice, and my joy. The rest wasn't just physical. It was about reconnecting with the reason I started leading in the first place."

Decoding the Silent Rules

Once I named the internal pressure, the emotional weight, the mask, the micro-tensions, the next layer hit me just as hard. There's a whole set of rules at play in leadership, and nobody hands you a manual. When you're a Black man in that space, you're not just expected to play the game, you're expected to master it without admitting you're playing.

I started noticing it early in my transition to senior leadership. I'd be in meetings where everyone already knew the decision had been made before we walked into the room. But we still had to "discuss it." That's when I realized: it's not about the meeting, it's about the hallway before the meeting. Power had already changed hands, and I hadn't been in the room when it happened. Or I'd give feedback with clarity and strategy, and it would be met with discomfort, because I wasn't using the right tone or "socializing" the idea beforehand. Meanwhile, others could challenge ideas with zero finesse and still be seen as bold or visionary.

That's when I learned: there are silent rules to how power moves. Rules like, it's not just what you say, it's who you say it to first. Rules like, your credibility is built behind the scenes before it ever shows up on paper. There's a silent rule that being right is not the same as being heard. And another: performance gets noticed, but politics gets you promoted.

None of that was in my onboarding binder, but it was everywhere in tone, in timing, in how decisions got made, and in how people protected their influence. And here's what made it even more complicated: the higher we rose in position, the more those rules were wrapped in politeness. It wasn't about being told "no", it was about being "looped out," or "deprioritized," or "restructured." It wasn't about being excluded, it was about being invited to a meeting after the decisions had already been made.

So I had to stop just doing the work. I had to start studying the room.

Understanding the unspoken rules of power didn't mean compromising who I was, it meant decoding the system so I could move with strategy, not just certainty.

It meant building relationships that weren't just comfortable, but consequential.

It meant learning how to carry influence that wasn't loud, but undeniable.

Because the truth is, if you don't understand the rules, you're not just at risk of being overlooked, you're at risk of being outplayed.

And the goal isn't just to survive the game; it's to learn it well enough to change it.

As you reflect, as you hold up this mirror, I often encourage my clients to take five intentional minutes to ask themselves:

- Who am I when nobody's watching?
- Where does that version of me go during the workday?
- What would it look like to lead from a place of truth, more often and more consistently?

Chapter 2:

The Silent Rules Of Power

The silent rules of power are the unspoken codes that govern how influence truly operates in leadership. They're not written in your employee handbook, and they're not discussed during performance reviews, but they shape everything: who gets access, who gets protected, who gets promoted, and even who receives the benefit of the doubt. They're the difference between performing and being perceived as ready. They separate simply doing your job from being seen as strategic.

I didn't learn these rules in a leadership seminar. I learned them the hard way, by losing power I didn't even realize I had until it was gone. One moment stands out. I had just wrapped up a major initiative, one that delivered strong results and high visibility. I presented the final analysis, made the case for scaling the work, and expected momentum to follow. The presentation went well, but the follow-up was silence. No traction, no movement, no next steps.

Weeks later, I discovered that another leader had already been quietly building consensus to take the project in a different direction. They had looped in key stakeholders before the final meeting even happened.

Learning the Game Behind the Game

That's when it hit me: I had been playing checkers while he was playing chess. He wasn't necessarily smarter. The outcomes weren't better. But he understood something I didn't, that power moves before the meeting, and decisions happen in whispers, not spotlights. Leadership is as much about positioning as it is about performance.

I started paying attention, not just to what people said, but how and when they said it. Who was always in the pre-meetings? Whose name was attached to success, even when they didn't do the heavy lifting? Who never seemed flustered because they already knew where the conversation was headed before it even started?

That's when I realized there's a visible side to leadership, metrics, milestones, mastery. And then there's the political side relationships, narrative, and influence.

Black men in leadership are often told to "just focus on the work," but the work alone isn't enough. You have to understand how power moves, even when no one says it out loud. Because if you don't know the silent rules, you're not underperforming, you're just under-informed.

And that's a setup. One that keeps talented, capable Black leaders stuck at the threshold, still wondering what they're missing.

I'm thinking about Julian, a senior director in the government space, working in Government Relations and Public Policy. Something he once told me stuck:

"Trust doesn't come from trying to fit in. It comes from showing up consistently, across meetings, across pressure, and across time. When people know what you stand on, they start standing with you. And that's how you lead the room, not just sit in it."

From Performance to Positioning

Once I understood the silent rules of power, my entire approach to leadership shifted. Before that, I believed my value lay in output, how much I produced, how polished my work was, how flawlessly I executed tasks. Excellence still matters, but I learned that in leadership, performance isn't enough if the politics around you are moving faster than the metrics in front of you.

Once I grasped how power actually works, I stopped trying to prove I belonged and started positioning my leadership. I began to move differently. For example, I stopped waiting for formal meetings to share bold ideas and started having pre-conversations with decision-makers, the ones who could advocate for me when I wasn't in the room. I began observing not just what was said, but what was left unsaid, reading body language, shifts in tone, and noting who got looped in early versus who was informed late.

I also became intentional about building strategic relationships across, not just up. Because in the rooms where power is negotiated, your peers' perception of you can be just as critical as your performance record. I stopped thinking I had to do everything to prove I was capable. Instead, I started aligning my voice with timing, influence, and audience. That's a silent rule too, when you speak matters just as much as what you say.

But here's the key: I didn't have to sell out to learn how to move smart. I didn't trade authenticity for access. I simply stopped assuming that being right was enough to be effective. Because once I understood the game behind the game, I realized leadership isn't just about impact, it's about leverage. And leverage requires insight. So now, when I enter a room, I ask myself:

- Who are the informal power brokers here?
- What conversations already took place before this meeting?
- Where can I create influence, not just offer input?

That's what changed. I stopped playing from the outside in and started leading from the inside out, with awareness, alignment, and unapologetic strategy.

One prompt I encourage clients to reflect on during their leadership journey is this:

- Where in your leadership are you overperforming but under-leveraging?

Executive Presence as Command, Not Costume

Executive presence is the mask, the measure, and the real move. It's often described as a mix of gravitas, communication, and appearance. But when you get real about what executive presence means in most corporate spaces, it's a code word. A catch-all for how comfortable you make others feel in your leadership.

For Black men, that comfort often has nothing to do with competence. You can be sharp, articulate, and data-backed, and still be labeled "too aggressive," "not quite ready," or "rough around the edges." So we're told, "Work on your presence," but the translation is: "Soften yourself."

What I've learned is that executive presence isn't about becoming someone else. It's about mastering how you carry who you are in high-stakes spaces. It's not a mask, it's command. Presence is what allows you to speak with authority without raising your voice. It's what makes people lean in, not because you're performing, but because you're anchored.

Once I learned the silent rules of power, I saw executive presence differently. It wasn't just about looking the part. It was about reading the room while staying rooted in myself. That looked like using intentional silence to give weight to my words. That looked like asking precise, surgical questions that shifted conversations without confrontation. It looked like managing not just my tone, but the timing of when I entered a conversation. And it looked like letting my calm carry just as much authority as my content.

The nuance is that executive presence is often taught from the outside in, Dress like this. Stand like that. Speak in bullet points. But for Black men, it has to come from the inside out. You can wear the right suit, have the perfect slide deck, and still be dismissed if you haven't done the work to own your voice and read the unspoken power dynamics around you.

Executive presence isn't just polish. It's discernment. It's alignment. It's the quiet edge that makes your leadership undeniable, even when they can't quite name why.

So yes, it matters. But don't confuse presence with performance. Presence without authenticity is just a costume. Real presence starts when you lead from conviction, not just composition.

"I had to stop mimicking executive presence and start defining it. When I showed up grounded in who I was, not just what I thought they wanted, I got more respect, not less. They didn't always like it. But they couldn't ignore it."

Derrick, SVP of Strategy & Operations, Global Tech Firm

Playing Politics Without Losing Your Soul

Leadership is political. That's not up for debate. Decisions are shaped through relationships. Access often outweighs ability, and perception, accurate or not, can determine your entire trajectory.

But the tension remains: how do you navigate that reality without compromising your identity? How do you engage with the politics of leadership without performing for approval or betraying your truth?

Early in my career, I believed politics were beneath me. I told myself, "I'll just let my work speak for itself." But what I learned is this: your work might speak, but it doesn't always echo, especially when you're the only one in the room who looks like you.

So, I had to reframe what leadership politics meant. Not as manipulation. Not as fake handshakes or selling out. But as strategic alignment, understanding the landscape so I could move with intention instead of frustration.

I began asking myself:

- Where are the pressure points in the system?
- Who are the real decision-makers, and who do they listen to?
- How can I lead in a way that builds influence without betraying my values?

I learned to manage up, not by kissing up, but by creating clarity. I learned how to challenge without triggering. And I learned how to hold my values while still playing the long game, because not every battle deserves the same energy.

The key is this: I never confused diplomacy with dishonesty. You can be strategic without being shady. You can build influence without becoming inauthentic.

You just have to decide, up front:

- What are my non-negotiables?
- What am I not willing to trade, for a title, a check, or a temporary seat at the table?

Because authenticity doesn't mean saying everything you think.

It means that everything you do say is true to who you are.

That's how you play the game, without becoming the game.

Once I understood the silent rules of power, I faced a new challenge: How do I stay real without being misread? Because the truth is, when you're a Black man in leadership, being real can come at a cost. Raise your voice just a decibel too high, and you're "aggressive." Push back on a flawed strategy, and you're "difficult." Show emotion, and you're labeled "unstable" or "unprofessional." Meanwhile, when others do the same, they're praised as "passionate," "visionary," "bold." Same behaviors, different interpretations. That's what makes authenticity feel like a risk , not because it's wrong, but because the room isn't always ready for it. If you're not careful, being real can be read as reckless, not because you lack skill, but because the space lacks cultural literacy.

I had to learn a skill that wasn't in the leadership books: How to balance truth with timing, realness with restraint, and conviction with calibration. Here's what that looked like for me: I stopped reacting and started responding. Just because I felt something didn't mean I had to say it in the moment. Sometimes, strategic silence was the most powerful move. I learned how to tell the truth without burning the bridge. I could say what needed to be said, clearly, directly, and with edge, without making it personal or performative.

I built a circle of safe spaces where I could be fully unfiltered, so I didn't explode in the wrong rooms. That gave me the strength to be real without becoming reckless. The lesson? Being real doesn't mean being raw. It doesn't mean abandoning discernment or dismissing consequences. It means leading from alignment, not for approval. It means showing up with your full self, not your unedited self, but your anchored self. Because recklessness isn't authenticity. It's unprocessed emotion masquerading as truth. And if we want to lead systems change, not just personal catharsis, we have to master the difference.

"I used to think being real meant saying whatever was on my mind. But growth taught me that being strategic with my truth made me more effective. I'm still real, but now, I'm also intentional."

Andre, Chief Legal Officer, Fortune 500 Fintech

As you continue your leadership journey, take a moment to reflect on the following questions:

- In which areas are you doing excellent work but overlooking the political dynamics that could enhance your influence?
- What strategic relationships should you cultivate ahead of the next important meeting?

- How can you remain authentic while being intentional about when and how you speak your truth?

Chapter 3:

Real Doesn't Mean Reckless

Authenticity is often mistaken for recklessness in leadership, especially when it comes from a Black man, because most leadership cultures aren't designed to hold truth and power in the same space. We've been conditioned to believe that real leadership is polished, composed, and neutral, that it belongs in bullet points, boardroom etiquette, or the language of the Harvard Business Review. So when a leader shows up clear, direct, and unfiltered, and especially when that leader is Black, honesty gets confused with hostility. Passion is mislabeled as anger. Conviction is misread as ego. And suddenly, being real becomes a risk.

The Trap of Shrinking Your Truth

The problem isn't authenticity. The problem is what people project onto it. I've sat in rooms where a white colleague could slam the table and be called fiery or driven. But when I spoke with calm intensity about the inequality in a promotion pipeline, I was told I was being divisive or too emotional, not because what I said was wrong, but because the realness of my presence disrupted the performance of the space.

24

That is the trap. If you internalize those reactions, you start to believe your truth is too much. You begin to shrink to keep the peace. You start editing yourself to be palatable instead of powerful.

Let's be clear: authenticity isn't recklessness. Recklessness is reaction without reflection. Authenticity is alignment with intention. It's not about saying everything you feel, it's about standing in what's true, even when it costs you your comfort. The real issue is that we live in systems uncomfortable with truth. We live in systems more accepting of performative leadership than principled leadership. When you lead from principle, especially as a Black man, your clarity will challenge people's complacency, and that's when you get labeled reckless. But we're not here to be manageable. We're here to be transformational. I remember something Tariq said to me during a coaching call. He was talking about a moment when he was called reckless, and he said:

"They called me reckless when I started telling the truth about our hiring process, which was failing Black candidates at the time. But I wasn't reckless, I was responsible with my power, my voice, and my people. Leadership isn't about playing it safe. It's about telling the truth with strategy."

You have to be strategic in how you lead, because that's what transforms the space.

Choosing Alignment Over Acceptance

Courage in leadership doesn't always look like a bold speech or a big protest in the moment. Sometimes, it's quietly refusing to betray your values, even when compliance would make things easier. I remember being asked to roll out a new policy change that disproportionately impacted frontline employees, many of whom were Black and Brown individuals. The decision had already been made at the executive level, and I was told to just message it "the right way." In other words, put a bow on something broken, make it sound good and get ahead of the backlash. But everything in me said no. Not because I wanted to rebel, but because I knew that silence is complicity. Leadership isn't about comfort; it's about clarity. So I took a risk in that moment. I brought data. I brought context. I brought stories from the people this policy would hurt. I offered alternatives, not complaints. And I said: if we move forward with this, we need to be honest about what it means and who it will harm.

Some people in the room looked at me like I'd lost my mind. One leader even pulled me aside afterward and said, "You've got to be more careful. You don't want to be seen as always pushing back." But I wasn't pushing back. I was pushing up, on truth, on accountability, and on leadership that actually leads.

The thing is, people will celebrate your courage when it's convenient. But the moment you challenge the system, they'll call it aggressive, divisive, or "not the right time." That's when you have to decide: am I here to be accepted, or am I here to be aligned? I've learned that real courage in leadership is rarely rewarded immediately. It often comes with friction, with isolation, with the tension of knowing you did the right thing, and still paid a cost. But I've also learned that silence has a cost too. And it's usually your integrity.

So I lead with this in mind: if I have to choose between being liked or being honest, I choose honest, with strategy, with respect, but without apology. Because leadership isn't about being loud. It's about being clear. And sometimes the clearest thing you can say is: "No. Not like this."

Courage Versus Compliance

The difference between courage and compliance is that leadership isn't always loud. Sometimes, it's quiet, subtle and internal. It's the moment you must choose between doing what's expected and doing what's right. Compliance keeps the machine running. It's following policy, protecting your position, or keeping your head down because "that's how it's always been done." It's staying silent in meetings where politics run deep and stakes are high, simply because you don't want to be labeled difficult or disruptive. Compliance is survival, dressed up as strategy.

Courage, on the other hand, isn't reckless defiance. It's choosing integrity over image. It's making decisions that may not be popular but are grounded in principle. It's risking proximity to power

27

in order to realign with your purpose. In practice, compliance asks, "How do I protect myself in this decision?" Courage asks, "What truths need to be protected, even if I'm the only one standing for them?"

I've made both kinds of decisions. I've complied to keep the peace, only to lose my own in the process. I've stayed silent in moments when I knew the right thing to say but feared the fallout. Every time I chose compliance over courage, it cost me, not in position, but in identity. Because when you lead from compliance for too long, you start questioning your instincts. You become someone who survives the room but never shifts it. But when you lead from courage, even if you're shaking while you do it, you build something deeper than credibility. You build trust. You build a legacy that says, *"I didn't just play the game. I showed up with integrity, even when it wasn't convenient."* The truth is, compliance might keep you safe. But courage will keep you whole, and in this game, staying whole is the win that outlasts the title. The more you lean into what wholeness means for you, the stronger you become in your leadership journey.

There's always an opportunity to look back and reflect on your experience in order to impact someone, whether in the moment, in that same group, or in a new group as you move forward.

Strategic Authenticity Without Compromise

Navigating situations where being real can put you at a disadvantage is one of the hardest balancing acts in leadership, especially when you know that speaking up could cost you politically, socially, or professionally. The truth most people don't want to admit is that there are moments when being fully real in the moment isn't wise. Not because you're wrong, but because the room just isn't ready. And if you're not strategic, your truth becomes a headline, not a lever for change.

I don't believe in being fake, but I do believe in being strategic with your authenticity. Because the goal isn't just to express yourself, it's to position your leadership for impact. When I sense the room isn't ready, I ask myself:

- What's the bigger win, venting my frustration or shifting the system?
- Is this the right room, or do I need to build a coalition before making this move?
- Can I plant the seed here and push the truth further in a smaller, more strategic conversation?

Sometimes that means holding the truth in tension, not suppressing it, but stewarding it. Other times, it means naming it calmly and clearly, without letting emotion be used against you. The leadership skill that doesn't get taught enough is knowing when to speak up in a meeting and when to make your move afterward. Not every battle is won in the boardroom. Some victories happen in follow-up emails, others in side conversations, or through aligning quietly with the right people before the next decision is made.

I've had moments when I paused, not because I lacked courage, but because I had a strategy. And I've had moments when I spoke anyway, because silence would have cost me more than the backlash. The key is: don't confuse silence with submission, and don't confuse strategy with fear. Being real doesn't mean being reckless, and being strategic doesn't mean being fake. It means knowing the value of your voice, and using it when it can move something, not just when it can make noise. Because it isn't just about expression. It's about influence.

I also encourage clients to reflect on two things when navigating the tension between courage and compliance:

- When was the last time you chose compliance over courage, and what did it cost you?
- What would you do differently now, knowing what you know?

PART 2:

RECLAIMING YOUR LEADERSHIP VOICE

Chapter 4:

Your Leadership Is Your DNA

Being real is only half the equation. The other half is knowing which version of yourself you're leading from, because the danger isn't just in pretending for the room. The real danger is when you've been pretending for so long that you forget what's real for you. That's why owning your leadership style and the values you stand for isn't optional, it's foundational. It's not branding. It's not optics. It's identity.

I had to learn this the hard way. For years, I adapted to what each role required, what each executive preferred, and what each space rewarded. Yes, I performed well, but I led like a chameleon. An effective, but disconnected, chameleon. Present, but not powerful. Until one day I asked myself: If the title were stripped away, would I still know who I am as a leader? That question changed everything.

I began identifying what I call my leadership DNA, the non-negotiables that define how I move, how I make decisions, and how I show up when the pressure hits. That includes my values: what I will and won't compromise for influence. That includes my style:

how I naturally lead when I'm not performing. And that includes my boundaries: what I protect to stay aligned and whole.

When you own your leadership DNA, you stop leading for approval and start leading from alignment. You stop mimicking what worked for someone else and start trusting what's already wired within you. This is the beginning of voice, not just vocalization, but vision. Because once you get clear on who you are, you don't just speak differently. You decide differently. You move differently. And most of all, you stop asking permission to lead like yourself. That's the most important thing: to step into a room and lead like yourself, because you are what's been missing from the room.

Uncovering Your Leadership DNA

Clarifying your leadership DNA is less about creating something new and more about returning to what has always been there. Your leadership DNA is the part of you that was never up for debate, only buried beneath layers of expectation. It's the most real, raw, and aligned version of your leadership identity, not the version you were taught to perform, but the one you genuinely believe in. It's your values, your instincts, your natural leadership rhythm when you're not managing perceptions or bracing for judgment.

Clarifying your leadership DNA means getting honest about your purpose, what you lead for. It's about embracing your natural style, how you lead best. And it's about identifying your non-negotiables, what you refuse to compromise. The key is this: you don't create your leadership DNA, you remember it. It has always been there. But for many of us, it's been shaped over, softened, or silenced by systems that reward only fragments of our leadership, never the whole.

For me, that process began when I hit leadership burnout, not just physical, but spiritual. I was in a role that looked successful on paper, but I felt hollow inside. I had been leading for optics, for outcomes, for survival, but not from truth. And I realized I had lost the sound of my own leadership voice. So I paused. I stopped chasing the next win.

I began what I now call a leadership audit. I asked myself: What energizes me as a leader, not just what I'm good at? When have I felt most connected to my team and purpose? What values do I keep returning to, even when they're inconvenient? And what kind of leader am I when I'm not afraid of the fallout?

I started writing those things down, not as a résumé or a brand statement, but as a personal code. What emerged were truths I had been living, but never naming. I lead with clarity, not chaos. I challenge people because I believe in their growth. I don't play politics; I build quiet power. And I refuse to lead in a way that costs me my peace.

Once I named those truths, I stopped mimicking leadership and started embodying it. That's what it means to clarify your leadership DNA. You stop asking, "What do they expect?" and start asking, "What does alignment look like for me, right now, in this role?" Because the real edge isn't found in comparison, it's found in clarity. And the clearer you are on who you are, the harder it is for anyone to move you off center.

I think about Julian, who works in public policy and government relations. He once said to me, *"You can't lead with consistency if you don't know what you stand on. I had to write my own leadership code, not the one they handed me, but the one that reflected my story, my people, my purpose."* That's when he stopped leading on autopilot. Many of us go through that same process, living on repeat, out of habit, stuck on autopilot. But once you become aware, you begin to operate differently.

From Survival Mode to Embodying Soul-Level Clarity

Defining your leadership style isn't about picking from a list of corporate buzzwords like "collaborative" or "results-driven." It's about uncovering the natural rhythm you lead from when you're not code-switching, second-guessing, or managing other people's expectations. It's the posture you carry when you're grounded. It's how you move when you're not trying to impress, just impact.

To be real, I didn't always know mine. For a long time, I led based on what I thought leadership was supposed to look like. I mirrored the executives around me, most of whom didn't look like me. I mimicked their tone, their tempo, their detachment from the human side of the work. And while I could play the role, it always felt off. I wasn't burnt out from the work; I was burnt out from the act.

The turning point came during a team restructure I was leading. It was high pressure, high visibility. I approached it the textbook way: strictly data-driven, emotions minimized, performance metrics front and center. And sure, the numbers looked great on paper, but my team? They were confused, disengaged, and anxious. I could feel it. They weren't responding to me, not because I lacked confidence, but because I lacked connection.

That's when I stepped back and asked myself: When have I been most effective, not just efficient? When have I felt most alive, most trusted, and most impactful as a leader? The answer: every time I led with transparency. Every time I pushed people with care, not control. Every time I named what others were afraid to say, but did it with dignity.

That's when I realized my leadership style is rooted in clarity, accountability, and emotional intelligence. I lead with transparency, even when it's uncomfortable. I demand excellence, but I make sure people feel seen as they rise to meet it. I hold people to a standard, but I also hold space for their humanity. I don't shy away from tension; I step into it to unlock growth and move people forward.

Once I named that, I felt free. I stopped trying to fit into someone else's mold. I stopped measuring myself against other people's styles. And I started building teams, driving strategy, and managing relationships in a way that felt fully mine. That's what defining your leadership style does, it gives you a compass in spaces that will always try to make you conform. And once you have that compass, even when the room is cold, the politics are thick, or the pressure is high, you don't lose your rhythm. You lead from it. I created a leadership worksheet that helps leaders reclaim the way they're already leading. It's a set of questions, four steps that walk you through a mindset shift away from checkboxes. Your leadership style isn't something you manufacture; it's something you remember. I guide people through this process to help them get really clear on how they naturally lead, when they're not performing, not proving, and not protecting themselves. You take the time to be honest and trust that your leadership style isn't missing. It's just been buried under years of managing perception.

Leadership Style Inventory: Reclaiming the Way You Lead

Use the Leadership Style Inventory worksheet as a mirror for your leadership, not a measuring stick. These prompts are designed to help you name, claim, and reclaim how you lead. Aim for honest clarity, not perfection. This is about alignment, not assimilation.

STEP 1: Core Values (What anchors you?)

- What are the top three values you refuse to compromise?
- Where did those values come from, life experiences, mentors, or pain points?
- How do these values manifest in your leadership style?

STEP 2: Leadership Identity (Who are you when no one's watching?)

- What makes your leadership voice distinct?
- In team settings, how do you naturally show up, as a visionary, builder, challenger, or stabilizer?
- Where do you find yourself shrinking, overcompensating, or performing?

STEP 3: Authentic Power Moves (How do you lead when you're in alignment?)

- What decisions or behaviors signal that you're leading from your truest self?
- What practices help you return to alignment when you've drifted?
- How do you recognize when you're compromising your leadership identity?

STEP 4: Non-Negotiables (What will you never trade for advancement?)

- What lines will you never cross, even if it costs you influence or access?
- What boundaries protect your peace and presence?
- What does "selling out" look like to you, and how do you avoid it?

This is your leadership inventory. It's not for your boss. It's not for your résumé. It's for you. Because the more you own your rhythm, the harder it becomes for anyone to push you off-beat.

Making Your Values Non-Negotiable Without Losing Influence

Knowing your values is one thing, but making them visible, consistent, and unshakable in leadership spaces? That's where the real work begins, and where true courage shows up. The truth is, every leadership culture will test your values. Some will do it subtly, by asking you to "massage the message" or "play the game a little longer." Others will do it overtly, expecting your silence when harm occurs or pressuring you to co-sign decisions that clash with your ethics.

Either way, the test is the same: Will you bend to stay in the room, or will you build credibility by standing in truth, even if it costs you something? I've learned that values aren't just personal; they're political. The clearer you are about them, the more you shift the room, without even trying. But to do that, you have to move from internal agreement to external declaration.

Internal Alignment to External Declaration

I can walk you through how I've done this, and how I've seen others succeed with it. It begins with four key steps. First, I name my values out loud from the start, whether I'm onboarding into a new role or stepping into a leadership transition. I state my values upfront. I let people know: I lead with transparency. I make decisions with equity in mind. I don't do politics at the expense of people. That doesn't just set the tone, it sets a boundary. It forces others to decide early on if they can respect the way I lead.

Second, I model my values in small moments, not just during big decisions. You don't prove your values in crisis; you prove them in how you show up every day. If I say I value accountability, I hold myself accountable first. If I claim to lead with empathy, I don't dehumanize people just to meet metrics. If I say truth matters, I don't hide behind optics when it's time to address hard things. People watch your values more than they hear them. If your actions don't echo your alignment, your words are just noise.

Third, I build boundaries around what I won't do. Many leaders skip this step, and it often leads to burnout. Every leader needs what I call non-negotiables: clear lines you don't cross, even when the pressure mounts. For me, those include: I won't lie to protect poor leadership. I won't stay silent to keep the peace if harm is happening. I won't mentor people within toxic systems I haven't challenged. These aren't just boundaries; they're guardrails that keep me from losing myself in the game.

The fourth thing is this: I let my values shape my legacy, not my reputation. Reputation is what people say when you're in the room. Legacy is what remains when you're no longer in the seat. I've had to ask myself, "Do I want to be remembered as someone who played the role well, or as someone who redefined what the role could be?" That question keeps my values sharp, because I'm not just leading for a promotion. I'm leading for the version of me I refuse to abandon.

I think about Malik, someone I've also worked with, who serves as a regional director in healthcare operations. During one of our coaching sessions, he said something that stuck with me: *"Your values have to show up in the hard calls, not just the mission statement. If people know what you stand for and they see you live it, then even your silence carries weight. But if you compromise too much, your presence loses its edge."*

When I work with clients in leadership roles, particularly those navigating the transition from mid-level to senior-level leadership, I encourage them to reflect deeply using these three prompts:

- What are three values I refuse to compromise in my leadership?
- What decisions or moments have tested those values?
- What boundaries do I need to re-establish so my leadership remains aligned with my truth?

There was a moment in my career, one of those pivotal leadership crossroads, when I had every reason to follow the script. A high-stakes partnership was on the line. The organization was under external scrutiny, facing pressure from the top, and fear was thick inside the walls. I was tasked with delivering a message to calm the waters and present a unified front. What they wanted was a performance. What I knew we needed was truth, not just any truth, but my truth. A message shaped by the story I carry.

So instead of crafting a polished message, I stepped into the room and shared something real. I told the people I was working with at the time what it meant to grow up being taught that you have to be twice as good to get half as far. I told them how it felt to be in leadership and still feel like my authenticity was a liability. I shared what I refused to replicate in this role: the kind of leadership that performs well in front of executives but leaves people feeling disposable behind closed doors.

I connected the business decision to something deeper, a personal ethic shaped by years of navigating spaces where silence was expected, but my story demanded a voice. Something shifted. The conversation became real, not defensive, not performative. People spoke from experience, not from policy. And the decision we made wasn't just strategic; it was aligned.

That moment taught me that my story wasn't a side note, it was a leadership asset. It wasn't something to hide until I earned credibility; it was how I built credibility in that moment. Because when you lead from your story, you lead from a place no one can fake. You bring a depth that data can't replicate. You build trust that can't be manufactured.

When your story is rooted in truth, not trauma, not ego, but truth, you shift the room without raising your voice. That's the power of leading from your story. It's not about centering yourself; it's about anchoring your decisions in something deeper than politics, performance, or fear. It's about showing up, not just as a title, but as a whole leader.

Leading When You're the Only One

Once you've done the internal work to clarify your leadership DNA, the next test isn't about how well you lead, it's about how steadily you lead. Especially when you're the only one in the room carrying your story, your lens, your lived experience. Let's be honest: it's one thing to be real in a room full of alignment. It's another thing entirely to stay grounded when you're surrounded by silence, skepticism, and side-eyes.

Being the only one doesn't just mean you're the only Black man at the table. It means you're the only one asking the questions others avoid. The only one naming what others are comfortable ignoring. The only one who feels the weight of what's unsaid while everyone else celebrates surface-level wins. That's when your leadership DNA gets tested, not in theory, but in practice.

For me, leading as one of the only ones in the room meant learning how to build quiet power. I stopped trying to match energy and started mastering presence. I stopped over-explaining my point of view and began anchoring in consistency. And I started using my story not as an emotional plea, but as a leadership lens that no one else could replicate. Because what I learned is this: you don't need backup to be bold. You don't need consensus to be clear. You just need to trust that who you are isn't a liability, it's your leadership advantage. So when you walk into that room as the only one, the goal isn't to shrink. It's not even to prove. It's to shift the atmosphere by standing flat-footed in who you are and letting your leadership speak before you even open your mouth.

"I stopped trying to prove I belonged and started leading like I did. Once I embraced being the only one as a position of

perspective, not isolation, my confidence changed. So did the room."

Andre, Chief Legal Officer, Fortune 500 Fintech

It really is about your perspective. When I stopped trying to prove I belonged and started leading like I did, when I embraced being the only one as a position of perspective, not isolation, my confidence shifted in every room I entered.

Here are a few questions I ask people to reflect on:

- Where have I been hiding my story in leadership spaces?
- What lessons from my journey have shaped how I make decisions today?
- What would shift if I led from those truths, not just from my resume?

Chapter 5:

Leading When You're The Only One

Being the only Black man at a leadership table is a strange mix of visibility and invisibility. You're highly visible, watched, interpreted, and overanalyzed. Every word carries weight. Every reaction is scrutinized. Even silence is noticed. You feel the tension of being the first and the only, whether it's acknowledged or not. And yet, at the same time, you're invisible. Your perspective isn't always invited. Your lived experience is rarely acknowledged. And when you do speak the truth, it's often met with discomfort, defensiveness, or a silence so loud it echoes after the meeting ends.

That's the duality. You're essential, yet expendable. Present, but alone. At the table, but never fully in the room. And that isolation isn't just professional, it's emotional. There are moments when you wonder: Am I here because they believe in my leadership, or because I check a box? If I speak up, will I be heard, or handled? And if I disappear, would anything about this space actually change?

I've been there. I've carried the weight in rooms where I had the title, the credibility, and the track record, but still felt like I had to audition for belonging. This is how I manage it. Because I don't think those feelings ever completely go away; it's about learning how to manage the emotions when you enter these spaces, and getting better at it over time.

First, I stopped waiting for the room to validate my presence. I started walking in already knowing: I belong here. Full stop. Not because of a DEI initiative or a quota, but because my leadership, my lens, and my lived experience add value that no one else at the table can replicate.

Second, I built what I call quiet power. I stopped performing and started observing. I learned how to influence through consistency, not volume. I let my leadership speak in spaces where explanations would only be exhausting.

Third, I stopped carrying the weight of representation like it was mine alone. Yes, I'm aware of the symbolic importance of being the only one in certain spaces, but I also refuse to let that pressure rob me of authenticity or joy. I represent, but I don't reduce myself to representation. I lead from a place of wholeness.

Because being the only one doesn't mean you're out of place. It means you're in position. And when you stop seeing your presence as a problem to solve, and start treating it as a power to steward, you move differently. You lead differently. And eventually, you shift the room so that someone else never has to be the only one again.

Building Quiet Power: Presence Without Permission

For Black men in leadership, building quiet power in spaces where you're the minority isn't just a leadership strategy, it's a survival skill and a strategic advantage. When you're the only one in the room, the fear is real: fear of being labeled aggressive for speaking up, fear of being too invisible and not visible enough, fear of saying the wrong thing, and having it become the thing people talk about after the meeting.

That fear creates two temptations: to shrink in order to stay safe, or to speak loudly just to prove your presence. But there's another path, one I call quiet power, and that's where real resilience lives. It's not about being silent; it's about being solid.

Quiet power is influence that's not performative, but undeniable. It's the calm authority that makes people listen, even when you're not the loudest. It's the way your presence shifts the energy in the room because you're rooted, not reactive. It's walking into spaces that weren't designed for you, and not asking for permission to lead anyway.

Here's how anyone can build quiet power in four steps:

First: Be consistent when the room is inconsistent. Quiet power comes from emotional stability under pressure. You don't have to react to every microaggression. You move with intention. You let your consistency speak louder than your defense. You don't need to clap back, your record is already clapping for you.

Second: Master discernment over display. You don't need to say everything you're thinking to be powerful. You ask sharp questions. You drop truth with timing. Quiet power knows when to wait, when to speak, and when to move behind the scenes to shift the room.

Third: Stay rooted in your leadership DNA. The most powerful leaders don't chase approval, they lead from clarity. You must know what you believe, how you lead, and what you won't compromise. When your leadership comes from identity, not insecurity, even your silence carries weight.

Fourth: Build influence before you need it. Power moves before meetings. Build strategic relationships across, not just up, and support others quietly. They'll start supporting you publicly. Quiet power isn't loud, because it doesn't need to be.

The opportunity for resilience here lies in understanding that being the minority doesn't mean you're powerless. It means your resilience becomes your presence. It means you develop a form of leadership that isn't dependent on being the center of attention; it's rooted in legacy thinking. Quiet power is what makes you unshakable when systems try to shake you. It's what transforms fear into focus and pressure into poise. Because when you carry quiet power, you stop proving, start positioning, and begin shaping the room, without needing to shout at it.

Andre, who works in fintech, once said to me: *"Quiet power is knowing you don't have to match the energy. I stopped reacting and started leading from alignment. That's when people stopped questioning me and started listening to me."*

When I think about the quiet power checklist, leading the room when the room wasn't built for you, quiet power isn't the absence of voice; it's the presence of alignment. I encourage leaders to use this checklist to reflect on how you're showing up in leadership spaces when you're the only one, or one of the few. These aren't "you should do this" items, but strategic self-checks designed to help you move with clarity, confidence, and calm authority.

Quiet Power Checklist: Leading When the Room Isn't Built for You

"Quiet power is not the absence of voice; it's the presence of alignment."

Use this checklist to reflect on how you're showing up in leadership spaces where you may be the only one, or one of the few. These aren't mandates or "shoulds"; they're intentional self-checks designed to help you lead with clarity, confidence, and calm authority.

1. Am I Leading with Alignment or Performing for Approval?

☐ I know what I believe, and where I won't compromise.

☐ I don't shape-shift to match the comfort level of the room.

☐ I choose timing and truth over reaction and reactivity.

"You don't need to be loud when your values are clear."

2. Am I Showing Up Consistently Across Rooms?

☐ I don't shrink in executive meetings, nor do I flex in team meetings.

☐ I communicate with calm, confident clarity, even under pressure.

☐ I allow my presence to speak before my performance ever does.

"Consistency builds credibility, especially when others expect you to fold."

3. Am I Building Strategic Relationships Behind the Scenes?

☐ I engage in pre-meetings and side conversations, not just public discussions.

☐ I identify who holds informal power and build trust with them.

☐ I offer quiet support, allowing my influence to grow naturally.

"Power doesn't always stand in the spotlight. It shapes who the spotlight shines on."

4. Am I Grounded in My Own Pace and Presence?

☐ I don't rush to respond just to prove I belong.

☐ I pause, breathe, and reflect before I speak.

☐ I bring calm into the room, not performative energy.

"Quiet power isn't passivity, it's practiced control."

5. Am I Investing in My Emotional and Cultural Resilience?

☐ I have safe spaces where I can process what the room isn't ready to hold.

☐ I remind myself that I'm not just representing, I'm anchoring.

☐ I carry my story with pride, not apology.

"You don't just carry the work. You carry the wisdom the room didn't know it needed."

Final Reflections:

- In what area of my life do I currently feel most anchored in my quiet power?
- Where am I still reacting instead of responding with intention and strategy?
- What is one shift I could make this week to lead from groundedness rather than reactivity?

From Representation to Real Influence

When I think about representation versus real influence, representation is visibility; influence is impact. Representation is being invited to the table. Influence is shaping what's on the agenda, and deciding who's in the room next. For clarity, representation matters, especially for Black men. Just being at the table can shift perceptions for those coming up behind us. Our presence alone disrupts the status quo. But it's also important not to confuse presence with power. You can have a seat, the title, the applause, and still not be moving anything that truly matters. That's the trap of tokenism dressed up as access. You're visible but voiceless. You're included but not consulted. You're celebrated but not taken seriously when it counts. And if you're not careful, you start mistaking representation for progress.

Real influence is when your voice changes things, not just echoes the safe party line. It's when your values guide decisions, your presence shapes culture, and your leadership opens doors, not just for yourself, but for others. You know you're walking in influence when you can say the thing no one else is saying, and it actually moves the room. People start coming to you before the meeting, not just nodding in agreement after it. You know you're walking in influence when your ideas outlive the slide deck. Your principles shift policy. You don't have to raise your voice to raise the standard. That's not just presence. That's power, stewarded well.

Where we get stuck is when we're told: You're the first. You're the role model. You're inspiring. And without realizing it, we start performing the idea of representation instead of building real leverage. We become the face of progress, not the force behind it. You don't get paid in exposure; you get paid in impact. Representation without influence is a photo op. Influence without performance is just a strategy.

So the challenge is this: Don't just be a symbol, shape the system. Don't just show up, shift something. Don't just represent, redefine what leadership looks like when it's rooted in truth.

I also encourage leaders to reflect on the following:

- Where am I settling for visibility without voice?
- What would it look like to turn my position into power I can pass on?
- Who benefits when I stay quiet?
- Who suffers when I don't lead fully?

I think about Tariq, a VP of People & Culture at a national nonprofit, whom I've mentioned before. He once said to me: *"Representation puts me in the room, influence keeps me in it. I had to stop trying to be impressive and start being effective. They saw me, but they didn't start listening until I moved from politeness to purpose."* I believe that's when real influence begins, when you ground yourself in purpose, rather than in the version of yourself you think others want to see. And I think that's also where the trap lies.

Carrying the Weight Without Being Crushed

If we're being real, being the only one at the table comes with a weight that most people don't see, and even fewer will name. You're not just there to lead; you're there to decode, defend, and often deliver beyond what the role requires. You carry the pressure to represent, the responsibility to speak up, and the emotional labor of protecting your peace while managing other people's comfort. It's heavy, and if you're not intentional, it will either make you shrink or make you harden.

What I've learned is that you can carry the weight without letting it define you. You can be the only one and still be whole. The way I balance it is by leading from alignment, not from expectation. I remind myself: I'm not here to play a part. I'm here to lead from my truth, my leadership DNA, my values, my story, my rhythm.

I don't have to chase credibility. I stopped performing representation and started building power. Being the only one doesn't mean I have to take on every fight, every burden, or every teachable moment. I pick my spots. I build alliances. I influence behind the scenes, because leadership isn't about carrying everything; it's about knowing what to carry on purpose.

I stay rooted in something bigger than the table. My worth isn't tied to the table; it's tied to the assignment. The moment I let the room shrink my vision, I start trading power for proximity. But when I stay grounded in the why behind my leadership, I can lead with clarity, even when I'm walking alone.

And the fourth area is this: I build spaces where I don't have to be the only one, especially outside the boardroom. I surround myself with people who get it. Other Black men I can exhale with. I mentor others, and that often extends beyond people who look like me, it's about being with people who understand. I also have mentors who remind me I'm not crazy. Because I don't just need professional allies, I need soulful mirrors who help me recalibrate.

The truth about this role is that being the only one is hard, but it's also holy. You're not just leading for a seat; you're leading for the shift. Every time you lead with authenticity, clarity, and courage, you make it easier for the person coming behind you to do the same, or do it better. So yes, the weight is real. But you don't have to carry it alone. And you don't have to carry it the way others expect you to. You get to carry it in your own rhythm, in your own voice, and in your own way, because authenticity isn't extra, it's your edge.

When you're the only one in the room, influence becomes survival, not just a strategy. And you quickly realize, you can't afford to lead by accident. But you also can't afford to lead from ego. Because ego will have you chasing validation instead of creating impact.

So the question becomes: How do you lead assertively without becoming performative?

For me, it started with one truth: Ego wants to be seen. Influence wants to be felt.

In rooms where I felt unseen or underestimated, I used to overcompensate. I'd talk more. Do more. Take up more space to prove I belonged. But all that energy wasn't coming from alignment, it was coming from insecurity.

Real influence began when I stopped leading to be impressive and started leading to be intentional. I stopped needing the room to recognize me and started making sure the room couldn't move without what I brought.

That shift required three specific things:

- Less performance. More presence.
- Less volume. More clarity.
- Less ego. More essence.

Because real leadership isn't loud. It's anchored.

The performative version of leadership tells you: stay polished, stay loud, stay visible. But if you're not careful, you'll build a brand people recognize, without the depth that actually changes rooms. Influence without ego is what separates performative leaders from transformational ones.

"I used to feel like I had to prove my worth in every meeting. Now I just lead from alignment and let the results speak. When you stop performing, your presence gets sharper. That's when people really start listening."

Derrick, SVP of Strategy & Operations, Global Tech Firm

Reflection Points for Leaders Navigating These Spaces

Whether you're transitioning from mid-level to senior leadership, or already in the senior seat:

- Where has the weight of being the only one made me shrink, harden, or perform?
- What would it look like to lead from wholeness instead of weariness?
- How can I carry the responsibility of leadership without carrying the system's dysfunction?

Chapter 6:

Influence Without Ego

There's a difference between being assertive and being performative. Every Black man in leadership has felt the tension between the two at some point. We're told to show up strong in the room, to project confidence. But when you're the only one, and all eyes are already on you, those expectations turn into a stage. Suddenly, leadership becomes performance. You say what's expected, not what's real. You speak in sound bites instead of with substance. You lead from optics instead of origin.

Over time, even your assertiveness starts to feel like a mask, loud on the outside, hollow on the inside. That's why I've learned that assertiveness isn't about volume; it's about alignment. It's about knowing what you stand on so clearly that you don't need to over-explain, over-compensate, or over-perform just to be heard.

Assertiveness Without Performance

What does assertive, non-performative leadership look like? It's rooted in clarity, not ego. When I speak, I'm not trying to win the room; I'm trying to move the conversation forward. I don't assert myself to prove I'm smart. I assert myself when the moment calls for truth, direction, or accountability. That's it, nothing extra.

This kind of leadership centers message over image. Performative leaders lead with the question: How will this look? I've learned to lead with: What needs to be said? What needs to shift? That shift alone saved me from chasing applause and helped me focus on impact. It listens first and speaks with precision. There's a quiet confidence that comes from not needing to dominate the room to influence it. I've learned to observe dynamics, read body language, catch the subtext, and then say something that shifts the room without shaking the table.

It doesn't flinch when the room doesn't clap. The performative trap is fueled by validation, but influence without ego doesn't need a round of applause. Sometimes, the most powerful thing you say won't be celebrated, it will simply be felt. Assertive leaders know how to sit in silence and still trust the truth they brought into the room.

I didn't always lead this way. There were times I chased credibility through charisma. I tried to own the room by sounding sharp, looking polished, playing the part. And for a while, it worked. But I noticed something: the more I performed, the more disconnected I felt from my why, and the less impact I made. Performance gets attention. But alignment creates traction. I had to slow down. I had to return to my leadership DNA. Stop talking to prove, start speaking to position my leadership where I could actually move something.

For leaders at this inflection point, I encourage reflection on these questions:

- Where have I been leading from performance instead of purpose?
- What would shift if I stopped needing validation to trust my voice?
- How can I be assertive without centering myself, only the mission?

The Strategic Power of Subtlety

Subtlety in leadership is often overlooked, especially in cultures that reward big personalities, bold declarations, and dominant presence. For Black men in leadership, subtlety has long been part of our power, not because we wanted to be invisible, but because we had to learn how to lead without triggering other people's bias.

Once I began to see subtlety not as suppression but as strategy, everything shifted for me. The truth about subtlety is that it isn't silence, it's surgical. It's how you shift a room without having to control it. It's how you create space for others to move while still anchoring your position. It's influence that moves with precision, not force.

In practice, this means knowing how to read the room before speaking into it. Subtle leaders don't need to dominate the space, they observe patterns, read nonverbal cues, sense emotional undercurrents, and then speak with intention. I've walked into rooms where saying too much would have cost me trust, so I listened. I offered one sharp insight and left an impact that outlasted the noise.

It's understanding when silence holds more power than sound. Silence isn't weakness. When used strategically, it disrupts. A pause at the right moment can shift attention. A question left hanging can expose flawed logic. Subtle leaders know how to let the room wrestle with truth without rushing to fill the silence.

In practice, this also means leading through presence, not pressure. Subtle presence doesn't shout for attention, it commands it through consistency, calm, and control. I've learned that when I'm grounded, I don't need to raise my voice or assert dominance. I let clarity carry the weight. People respond to that energy because it's steady, not showy.

There are ways to master subtlety. You must know your message so well that you don't need to oversell it. When your leadership is rooted in truth and alignment, theatrics become unnecessary. Subtle leaders don't perform their position, they embody it.

Another way to master subtlety is to cultivate presence before entering the room. Before high-stakes conversations, I don't rehearse a script, I center myself. I get quiet. I align with my purpose. That way, when I speak, it comes from depth, not defense.

The third way to master this is to trust stillness. Stillness doesn't mean passivity. Still leaders are powerful leaders, when their stillness is intentional. When your energy is clear, your values anchored, and your vision focused, subtle leadership feels like gravity in the room. You draw people toward clarity, not chaos.

Subtle does not mean soft. It means being sharp enough to move without making a mess. It means you don't need to win the volume war, because your vibration is already doing the work. This is how Black men have led for generations: with wisdom, with calm, with a heat that doesn't need the spotlight to burn through the noise.

"Subtlety is how I protect my power. I used to think I had to match energy to be taken seriously. Now I know: stillness is its own signal. When I stop chasing the room and start reading it, I lead it better."

Malik, Regional Director, Healthcare Operations

There was a moment in my career when everything in me wanted to speak up, loudly. A senior leader had made a public decision that undercut a strategy I'd spent months building and socializing. I wasn't just disappointed; I was furious. I had worked so hard to build consensus and secure buy-in. The team looked to me for a reaction. The room expected me to either explode or retreat. I did neither. Instead, I paused. I didn't match the energy; I matched the intention. I calmly asked one question that redirected the entire conversation: *"Can you help me understand how this aligns with the original outcome we committed to, especially around equity and long-term impact?"*

No emotion. No defensiveness. Just disciplined clarity. The room fell silent. What I did in that moment wasn't challenge the person, I challenged the alignment. I brought the conversation back to values, not ego. And in doing so, I asserted influence, without raising my voice.

After the meeting, two other leaders, one of whom had remained silent throughout the entire discussion, approached me and said, "I'm glad you said that." They shared that they had felt the same way but didn't know how to bring it up. That's when I realized: you don't have to be loud to lead. Sometimes, your greatest leadership moment is measured, not magnified. It's in what you don't say, what you don't escalate, and how you stay anchored when everything around you is pushing you to react.

What made that moment work was that I stayed aligned with the bigger mission, not just the emotions of the moment. I protected my leadership credibility by elevating the conversation instead of making it personal. I used a calm question to bring the heat without scorching the room. That's the edge. That's influence without ego.

It's the kind of leadership that doesn't need theatrics to be effective, just truth, timing, and presence.

There's a duality in leadership: sometimes you show up a little louder, other times a little quieter, and you get to choose those moments. But what I encourage leaders to reflect on, especially when they're considering doing the opposite of how they normally show up, is this:

- When have I tried to assert myself through volume instead of presence?
- What tools do I have to lead with calm clarity, especially in high-pressure moments?
- What would it mean to let alignment speak louder than performance in my next leadership challenge?

When you truly sit with those questions, you'll begin to realize just how powerful quiet power really is.

Ego Versus Influence

The real difference between ego and influence is this: ego wants to be seen; influence wants to be felt. Ego shows up needing validation. It craves credit. It wants to win every room, own every idea, and be recognized for every contribution. Influence, on the other hand, shows up through alignment. It doesn't need to prove; it needs to position. It understands the work is bigger than personal applause. It knows that real leadership isn't about being at the center, it's about creating a movement that outlasts your presence. When you're leading from ego, you talk more than you listen. You react to everything. You aim to dominate, not just contribute. Your self-worth rises and falls based on how others respond. Ego-driven leadership confuses power with control. Ego is loud, because it's fragile. And in leadership, fragility always costs you influence.

But when you're leading from influence, you observe first and speak with precision. You don't chase every battle, you choose the ones that matter. You hold steady when the room gets loud. You lead with presence, not posture. Your impact isn't measured by the spotlight, it's measured by what shifts. Influence is quiet because it's anchored.

My turning point in understanding the difference between ego and influence came when I found myself in rooms where I desperately wanted to make a point. I over-talked and under-listened. I left feeling heard, but not respected. Seen, but not trusted. Then I started moving differently. I stopped performing. I stopped chasing the mic. The less I tried to take control, the more the room leaned in when I spoke. Because I wasn't leading from ego anymore, I was leading from essence. During a one-on-one coaching session, Tariq said to me,

"When I was younger, I thought leading meant making sure everybody knew I was in charge. Now I know leadership is when

people feel clarity, even when you're not saying much. Ego demands attention; influence earns respect."

For leaders who find themselves at the crossroads, trying to discern whether they're leading from ego or from influence, I challenge you to sit honestly with your own leadership style and DNA, and ask:

- Where have I led from ego, and what did it cost me?
- What does it feel like when I'm moving from true influence?
- How can I strengthen my leadership presence without performing for approval?

When I think about influence that leads to impact, it's about alignment that delivers. Influence is powerful, but without aligned outcomes, it stays theoretical. Real leadership happens at the intersection of purpose and performance. That means your values aren't just personal, they're measurable. Your leadership isn't just rooted in authenticity, it's accountable.

When you align your leadership purpose with outcomes that matter, you stop being the inspiring leader people admire from a distance and start becoming the effective leader they trust to get things done.

Here's why alignment and metrics matter: I've seen too many Black leaders, specifically Black men in leadership, get boxed into the role of "moral compass" or "cultural voice in the room" while being sidelined when it comes to driving results. The trap is this: you either become the fixer of people's feelings, or you burn yourself out trying to prove you can both lead and deliver. But you don't have to choose between purpose and performance. You just have to align them.

When I got clear on my leadership purpose, who I serve, how I lead, and why it matters, I also got clear on my metrics:

- What does success look like beyond the spreadsheet?
- How am I holding people to high standards without compromising humanity?
- How do you tie performance to equity, innovation, and long-term value?

That alignment changed everything in my leadership journey. I wasn't just inspiring people, I was building a culture that performed. I wasn't just being real, I was results-driven without losing my rhythm.

Here's the shift in practice: When you lead from alignment, you measure what you say matters. You hold your team, and yourself, to a standard that reflects your purpose, and you create impact that is both felt and proven. You're not just leading for optics; you're leading for outcomes without compromising who you are. That's the mark of transformational leadership: clarity with results, conviction with receipts, and presence with measurable progress.

When I say you measure what you say matters, it's like a leadership truth serum. It means that if you claim something is important, whether that's equity, culture, team health, trust, or purpose-driven work, but you don't track it, prioritize it, or build accountability around it, then it's just talk. In other words, your values aren't real unless they show up in your metrics.

In practice, as a leader, if you say team well-being matters but only measure output and not burnout rates, then well-being doesn't truly matter in your leadership framework. If you say equity matters, but you're not tracking promotion rates, pay equity, retention across demographics, or who's in the pipeline, then equity is just a value on paper, not in practice. If you say innovation matters, but every idea has to be safe, approved by consensus, or data-proofed to death, then innovation isn't genuinely part of the culture.

The deeper point is this: what you measure is what you legitimize. That's how leadership cultures are shaped, not by the mission statement, but by what gets rewarded, repeated, and resourced. When I say something matters as a leader, I'd better be ready to measure it, not just to prove it to others, but to hold myself accountable to the kind of leadership I claim to represent. Because in the end, if you're not measuring the impact, it will come back to haunt you.

A Reflection Prompt for Leaders: Measure What Matters

Ask yourself these three questions:

- What outcomes define success for me, not just for the organization, but for my actual leadership legacy?
- Where do I need better alignment between my values and what I'm actually measuring?
- How can I move from performance for approval to performance from purpose?

PART 3:

THE AUTHENTIC PERFORMANCE MODEL

Chapter 7:

Aligning With Purpose And Metrics

Purpose isn't soft, it's strategic. If you're a Black man in senior leadership, or on your way there, you already know the pressure: deliver results, prove your value, drive outcomes. Deliver. Deliver. Deliver. You've likely felt the unspoken message: your purpose is powerful, but don't let it interfere with your performance. The translation is clear, keep your values in check, don't challenge what's being measured, and if it can't be tracked in a spreadsheet, keep it to yourself.

But here's the truth: purpose isn't a distraction from performance, it's the engine of sustainable performance. The problem isn't that we care too much. It's that we haven't been given permission to tie what we care about to what the business defines as success. So we end up disconnected. We lead teams but feel misaligned. We produce outcomes but don't feel ownership. We deliver results, but we're not delivering on our calling.

Aligning purpose with performance metrics is a leadership edge. I began integrating my leadership purpose with the metrics that define success in executive roles in three key ways.

First, I got clear on what success looks like for me, not just quarterly goals or KPIs. I asked:

- What kind of culture do I want to build within any organization I serve?
- What kind of leader do I want to be remembered as?
- How does my purpose show up in how I measure growth, trust, excellence, and equity?

That helped me design metrics that mattered, both to the business and to my legacy.

Second, I translated purpose into performance language. I stopped expecting people to value my why without connecting it to their what. If I cared about equity, I demonstrated how it impacts retention and brand credibility. If I cared about culture, I showed how team engagement drives innovation and reduces turnover. Essentially, I began speaking in results, without abandoning my roots.

Third, I created a scorecard that reflected my leadership values, which I often coach clients to do. If I said psychological safety mattered, I tracked it. If I claimed career development was a priority, I measured what was actually growing, not just who was performing, because what gets measured gets done. I refused to let purpose remain invisible.

For Black men in senior roles, many of us reached our positions by producing results. But we're rarely asked what purpose those results were tied to, even though we're performing at a high level. Now that we're at the table, we don't just need to deliver, we need to redefine what performance looks like through a culturally grounded lens. One that makes space for both strategy and soul. One that proves you can be purpose-driven and metric-aligned without shape-shifting to fit into the system.

I remember Julian, a senior director in government relations, saying during a coaching call:

"I started tracking what I said mattered, culture, retention, equity, and promotion, and suddenly, they couldn't ignore it. My purpose stopped being seen as a passion project. It became performance data, and that changed the game."

Turning Values into Visible Impact

I often encourage my clients, or anyone aiming to move from mid-level to senior-level leadership, to reflect on these prompts:

- What metrics have I inherited that don't truly represent my leadership purpose?
- Where do I need to redefine success in a way that aligns with my values?
- What would it look like to lead with both purpose and proof?

Purpose to Performance Scorecard: Turning Values into Visible Impact

"If they only measure what you do, but not who you're becoming or how you're evolving, then you need to bring your own scoreboard."

This tool helps you align your leadership purpose with the outcomes you're expected to achieve, without compromising your authenticity or your values. Think of it as a framework for developing your own leadership performance language, one that connects legacy with measurable results.

STEP 1: Define Your Leadership Purpose

Begin by articulating your clear and unapologetic why, the deeper reason you choose to lead.

- Leadership Purpose Example: To build high-performing teams rooted in equity, truth-telling, and personal growth so people can lead from their full identity, not just their job description.

- My Leadership Purpose: _____

STEP 2: Identify Your Core Values

List or circle 3–5 non-negotiable values that consistently guide your leadership:

- Core Values to Consider: Equity, Transparency, Accountability, Psychological Safety, Innovation, Legacy, Cultural Intelligence, Integrity, Spiritual Grounding, Collaboration, Trust, Growth
- Core Values I Lead From (Example: Equity, Accountability, Psychological Safety, Legacy):

STEP 3: Tie Each Value to a Measurable Outcome

This is where purpose meets performance. For each core value, ask yourself:

How can I measure whether this value is actively reflected in my leadership?

Value	What It Looks Like in Action	How I Will Measure It
Equity	Equitable access to development and promotion	% of underrepresented team members in leadership roles
Accountability	Clear expectations and mutual follow-through	Frequency of 1:1 check-ins and missed deadlines

Psychological Safety	People can challenge ideas without fear of backlash	Employee pulse scores, anonymous feedback themes
Legacy	Investing in next-gen Black leaders	# of mentees developed, sponsorships created

Weekly Reflection Question:

Am I leading in a way that reflects my values, and is that reflection visible in the outcomes?

STEP 4: Build Your Quarterly Leadership Scorecard

Use this template to track how well your actions align with your values over time:

Leadership Priority	Value Backing It	Key Metric	Progress (Y/N or %)	Notes / Adjustments
Build inclusive team culture	Equity and Safety	Inclusion pulse score	74% this quarter	Need to address drop in psychological safety
Develop future leaders	Legacy	Internal promotions	2 team members promoted	Track feedback from

				development sessions
Improve team clarity	Accountability	Missed deadlines	3% missed this quarter	Add performance rhythm to standups

Final Reflections:

- What Story Is My Leadership Data Telling?
- Where is my leadership in alignment with what I say?
- What am I not measuring that I should be?
- What might shift if I began sharing this scorecard with my team or peers?

Remember: If you don't define your own leadership metrics, someone else will, and their definition will rarely reflect your true purpose.

This scorecard isn't about proving yourself; it's about building a kind of leadership where results and values coexist.

- Where your influence leaves evidence.
- Where your legacy comes with receipts.

Leading From the Middle of the Tension

As a Black leader, the gap becomes even more pronounced. You might be labeled as passionate, inspirational, or culturally insightful, yet overlooked when it's time to make real decisions.

That's why, as a leader, you must lead from the middle of that tension, not diluted, not divided, but integrated.

Leading with both means hitting your numbers and checking the human cost of getting there. It means advocating for your team's well-being with the same energy you push for results. It means designing strategies that serve the business while advancing equity. You measure trust and safety, not just productivity. And you mentor people for roles that don't even exist yet, because your impact is future-minded.

When you lead with both impact and outcomes, people stop seeing you as just a performer, and start seeing you as a force.

For leaders navigating this space, reflect on these three prompts:

- Am I leading in a way that delivers both results and resonance?
- Where am I overemphasizing one and neglecting the other?
- What would I change if I designed every strategy with both metrics and mission in mind?

As you sit with those questions, lean into your values as a leader, and center yourself there.

Culture is the Compass, Not the Costume

For Black men in leadership, we're often told to adjust our presence to fit a dominant culture that never adjusted for us. But culture is the compass, not the costume. Black men in leadership have often seen culture treated like a side dish: something to sprinkle in when convenient, but never the main course. You can show it during celebration months, but not let it shape how you lead. You can bring your voice, but only if it's been polished to match the room. That's how we learned to code-switch, to survive, to be accepted, and to avoid making others uncomfortable.

The truth is, culture isn't what gets in the way of effective leadership. It's what makes leadership effective, when it's aligned. Culture shapes how we build, how we lead, and how we trust. Our cultural lens teaches us to lead with rhythm, not just rigidity. It shows us how to read people between the lines, and how to build loyalty through storytelling, respect, and truth. It teaches us to lead from intuition and emotional intelligence, because survival taught us to feel the room long before we were allowed to speak in it. That's not "soft skills." That's sacred leadership intelligence. When you code-switch away from that, you don't just lose your edge, you lose your center.

So how do you lead without code-switching? There are three specific ways:

First, name your cultural assets. What leadership styles stem from your upbringing, your community, your faith, your people? Don't dilute them, design around them. If you build trust through storytelling, don't save it for later, lead with it. If you communicate best with direct clarity and collective care, weave that into your leadership model.

Second, refuse to translate your humanity for someone else's comfort. You can speak in ways others understand without erasing yourself. You can adapt without performing, because leadership is about clarity, not camouflage.

Third, build cultures that reflect you, not just tolerate you. The goal isn't to be the exception. The goal is to shift the system so that your leadership style becomes the norm, not a niche. That's legacy work.

Why this matters: if you have to code-switch to succeed, then success will always cost you something sacred. Over time, that cost becomes burnout, disconnection, self-doubt, even resentment, because you built something impressive on top of an identity you weren't allowed to fully express. When you lead from culture, not in resistance, but in resonance, you stop negotiating your presence; you start commanding it. Because when culture and leadership align, you stop managing perception and start multiplying trust.

For individuals navigating this space, I leave you with three prompts:

- Where in my leadership am I still shape-shifting to match dominant culture?
- What cultural practices, instincts, or values do I need to reclaim as strategic?

- What would leadership look like if I stopped editing and started embodying?

For most of my leadership career, I was taught that creating clarity around performance meant being rigid, removed, and "professional", which translates to: don't show emotion, don't be too human, don't bring your story, bring the spreadsheets. But here's what I know now: Clarity doesn't require you to lose your authenticity. It requires you to lead with intention, not impression.

Honestly, when you're a Black man in leadership, the moment you set standards or drive accountability, you risk being labeled too intense, not collaborative, or hard to work with. So the temptation is to soften your standards or water down your delivery, but that's not leadership. That's survival. And survival can't scale.

What authentic clarity looks like is three things:

One, set expectations early and tie them to values, not just goals. I don't just tell my team what I expect; I explain why it matters. I say: We hold this standard because it reflects our excellence, our community, our legacy. That way, the performance bar isn't cold, it's cultural.

Two, communicate directly, but in your own voice, not someone else's tone. I've learned to give feedback the same way I give respect: with calm and care. I don't have to mimic corporate jargon or emotionally detach to be taken seriously. I just need to be grounded and consistent.

Three, build accountability as a culture, not a surprise. When clarity is woven into daily rhythms, not dropped only when there's a problem people understand the expectations. Because they trust who I am, they can trust what I ask of them.

The key is that authenticity isn't the enemy of clarity, it's the engine behind it. When people know you're consistent in your values, honest in your expectations, and rooted in something deeper than ego, they'll listen, even when it's hard, even when they disagree. Your authenticity earns you the space to challenge, correct, and raise the bar.

If you're navigating the transition from mid-level to senior leadership, ask yourself three things:

- Am I diluting clarity in order to stay liked or feel safe?
- Where have I sacrificed authenticity for structure, or structure for authenticity?
- How can I lead with bold expectations that still reflect who I truly am?

You can't lead what doesn't trust you. You can hold the title, hit the numbers, and say all the right things. But if you haven't built trust, real trust you're not leading; you're managing perception. When you're a Black man in a high-stakes leadership role, I think that's the trap. You're expected to deliver results and prove you're not a threat. You're expected to build consensus and keep your voice in check, to challenge broken systems, but not too loudly, not too soon, not too real. In that context, trust becomes your greatest currency, not just to protect yourself, but to activate your influence.

There are layers to trust in high-stakes environments where power is concentrated and politics run deep. Trust must be earned, not assumed. But there are nuances.

Trust isn't built by being agreeable. It's built by being consistent. If people know where you stand, they'll begin to lean on you, even if they don't always agree with you. Trust isn't gained through perfection. It's gained through presence. Your team doesn't need a flawless leader. They need one who shows up with integrity, listens deeply, and follows through. Trust isn't built in reaction; it's built in rhythm. People trust what they can count on, your tone, your values, your standards, your care. If those things change based on who's in the room, your leadership becomes unstable, even if your intentions are solid.

This is how I've built trust, especially in spaces where the stakes are financial, reputational, political, and cultural. You build trust by doing three things consistently.

First, tell the truth early, even when it's not polished. People trust clarity more than they trust charisma. In fast-moving environments, don't wait until everything is perfect. Share the truth with context, then lead the way forward.

Second, own your mistakes without losing authority. Accountability is a trust magnet. The moment your team sees you take ownership without deflection, they know they can follow you into complexity.

Third, protect people's humanity while raising the standard. The highest-performing leaders are those who stretch others without stripping their dignity. You build trust when your leadership leaves people feeling seen, safe, and sharpened.

Here's why trust matters more than ever: In systems that often perceive Black leadership through the lens of threat or tokenism, trust becomes your bridge. It's how you earn influence without ego. It's how you lead diverse teams without watering down the truth. It's how you challenge upward without being dismissed as defensive. It's how you build cultures that don't just perform, but transform and belong to something deeper. Because people don't follow titles. They follow truth-tellers they trust.

I'm reminded of a conversation I had with Evan, an executive coach and former COO in the education space. During a coaching session, he said something that stuck with me:

"I stopped trying to be the most impressive person in the room and started being the most consistent. That's when people started trusting me with the real stuff, the decisions, the conflict, the risks. Because trust isn't about who talks the best. It's about who shows up the same under pressure."

For anyone navigating leadership, reflect on these questions:

- Where in your leadership have you earned trust, and how?

- Where have you confused likability with trustworthiness?
- What would shift if you stopped trying to be seen as safe and started leading as someone worth trusting?

Chapter 8:

Building Trust In High- Stakes Spaces

When you're in a high-stakes leadership role, especially as a Black man, you're constantly navigating the balance between performance, perception, and power. You must deliver results upward, collaborate across teams, and still maintain the trust of those you lead. Amid all that, you're also working to stay aligned with your values, your culture, and your voice.

Let's be clear: managing up and across isn't about pleasing people. It's about positioning your leadership with clarity, consistency, and credibility. Here's what I've learned throughout my leadership journey:

- You can earn trust without chasing validation.
- You can build influence without becoming invisible.
- You can lead boldly without being branded a threat.

But you need a strategy, because the room won't always reward your presence.

Managing Up Without Compromising Down

How do you manage up in high-stakes spaces? I break it into three core strategies:

1. Lead with outcomes, not opinions.

When speaking to senior leaders, anchor your insights in what matters to them, business risk, impact, efficiency, brand, and people. Don't just say, "We need more support." Instead, say, "Here's the risk to team performance if we don't prioritize X, and here's what we stand to gain if we act now." That shift makes your leadership harder to overlook.

2. Communicate with calm confidence, not over-explaining.

Managing up doesn't mean shrinking yourself. It means speaking with clarity, not insecurity. Keep your tone steady, your points focused, and your timing intentional. Don't flood the room with words, flood it with insight.

3. Anticipate, then activate.

The best way to earn trust from above is to solve problems before they surface and bring solutions, not just concerns. Frame issues in the language of strategy, not emotion. Make it easy for leaders to say yes because you already think like one of them.

How do you manage across without compromise?

Again, three strategic approaches apply:

1. Build coalitions, not cliques.

Cross-functional trust is earned through shared wins, not personal alignment. Make it your priority to understand what your peers are measured on, and help them succeed. They'll remember that when it's time to support your next bold move.

I often coach newer managers and early-career leaders to build relationships across departments. Most people stay in their lane, but high-impact leadership means reaching across boundaries to form meaningful, cross-functional connections.

Second, don't lower your standards just to keep the peace. You can disagree without creating division. Say the hard things, but say them in a way that encourages reflection, not retaliation. This isn't about being liked; it's about earning respect across the entire system.

Finally, stay consistent, even behind closed doors. The fastest way to lose cross-functional trust is by saying one thing in a meeting and another behind the scenes. Let your leadership remain steady in the hallway, the group chat, and the boardroom. That kind of consistency builds credibility faster than charisma ever could. To hold it all together: confidence plus clarity plus consistency equals trust.

- Confidence says, "I know who I am and what I bring."
- Clarity says, "Here's what I need and why it matters."

- Consistency says, "You'll get the same leader no matter who's in the room."

That's how you manage up, across, and forward, without losing yourself.

That's how you lead with both strategy and soul in high-stakes spaces.

Respect vs. Validation: Know the Difference

Respect is built. Validation is chased. You just have to know the difference.

Early in my career, I didn't understand the difference between being respected and being validated. I believed that if I got the shout-out, the head nod, the glowing performance review calling me a "team player," that meant I was leading well. But here's what I learned the hard way:

Validation is performance-based. Respect is principle-based.

Validation is conditional. It depends on how comfortable, agreeable, or non-threatening you make others feel. Respect, on the other hand, is rooted in your consistency, your competence, and your character. It's earned when people realize you don't sway with the wind, you lead from alignment.

Seeking validation looks like over-explaining your decisions so no one misinterprets you. It's avoiding conflict just to keep the peace. It's downplaying your wins so you don't intimidate others. It's adjusting how you speak depending on who's in the room. It's feeling like you have to earn your place again, every time you open your mouth. That's not leadership. That's emotional debt. And it's exhausting, because no matter how much validation you get, it never feels like enough.

Earning respect means saying less, but making every word count. You don't chase applause; you seek alignment. You push back with clarity, not emotion, because you're grounded in truth. You hold your standards steady, regardless of power dynamics. And you leave the room without second-guessing yourself, because you know you didn't fold.

Here's the thing about respect: you might not get instant approval. You might make people uncomfortable. But over time, they'll trust you, not because you're performing, but because you're leading with integrity and focusing on outcomes, not optics.

This matters deeply for Black men in leadership. We've been taught to seek validation for survival: " Don't come off too strong," "Make people feel safe," "Be twice as good, and smile while doing it." But the truth is, if you keep leading for validation, you'll never lead fully. Your leadership will always be up for debate.

Earning respect means letting go of the need to be liked in order to be effective. It means trusting your voice, even when the room doesn't clap. It means being consistent, not just compliant.

Because the kind of respect that lasts, the kind that shapes systems, unlocks opportunities, and builds legacy, isn't handed out. It's embodied.

Andre, a chief legal officer in the fintech space, once said to me, *"Validation felt good, until I realized I was addicted to it. I needed someone to always affirm that I belonged. But once I started trusting my own standards, I no longer needed permission to lead. I just led. Respect followed."*

That stuck with me. I began encouraging my clients, especially those learning to move beyond the need for validation, to ask themselves:

- Where in my leadership am I chasing validation instead of standing in conviction?
- What might shift if I trusted my internal standard over external approval?
- How do I want people to respect me, and what am I doing to earn that respect without performing for it?

Respect vs. Validation Checklist:

Are you leading from conviction or from a need to be confirmed?

This checklist is designed to help you self-assess how you're showing up in high-stakes spaces. The goal isn't perfection; it's awareness and re-centering.

1. Why Did You Speak Up in That Meeting?

☐ I had something strategic to contribute. (Respect)

☐ I wanted to be seen as valuable or impressive. (Validation)

2. How Did You Handle Pushback?

☐ I stood firm in my point and welcomed the tension. (Respect)

☐ I softened my stance or backpedaled to avoid discomfort. (Validation)

3. How Are You Measuring Your Leadership Success Right Now?

☐ By my values, the outcomes I drive, and the impact I create. (Respect)

☐ By the amount of praise or positive feedback I receive. (Validation)

4. When You Challenge Upward, What's Your First Concern?

☐ Staying true to the mission and safeguarding the work. (Respect)

☐ Avoiding conflict and preserving favor with others. (Validation)

5. After a High-Stakes Conversation, What's Your Internal Dialogue?

☐ Did I lead with clarity and consistency? (Respect)

☐ Did they like me? Did I overshare? (Validation)

Reflection Scorecard

Tally your results:

- Mostly Respect responses? You're leading from alignment, keep anchoring.
- Mostly Validation responses? Time to realign your leadership with your truth, not their applause.

"Respect is quiet. Validation is noisy. One builds legacy. The other burns you out."

Vulnerability as Strategic Strength

For a long time, I believed that strength in leadership meant keeping everything tight, no cracks, no emotions, no doubts. Just competence, composure, and control. As a Black man in leadership, I was already under a microscope. The fear was real. I constantly questioned: If I showed too much emotion, would I be labeled unstable? If I shared uncertainty, would they question my readiness? If I opened up, would I be mishandled?

So, I started to build walls. I polished a mask. And it worked, until it didn't. Because what I learned the hard way is this: if people can't feel you, they won't follow you. They might respect your skill, they might nod in meetings, but trust is born in the spaces where strength and honesty coexist.

The balance is strength with discernment. Vulnerability isn't about emotionally dumping. It's not about telling everything. It's about strategic transparency, sharing what's real in a way that builds connection, not confusion. Strength isn't about perfection. It's about presence under pressure. It's about owning your truth and still moving the room forward.

When you balance the two, you acknowledge that you don't have every answer, but you're still leading with vision. You admit the pressure is real, but it hasn't broken your purpose. You model what it means to lead human-first, without being fragile.

How I practice balance is, first, by choosing my moments intentionally. I don't share vulnerability just to relieve my stress—I share it to deepen connection. That means I check my intentions first. I often ask myself: Am I sharing to build trust, or am I hoping to be rescued? My answer determines how I choose the moment.

Second, I name the pressure without transferring it. I might say, "This is a heavy lift. There's uncertainty, but we're not stuck. We're moving forward." That lets my team know they're not being gaslit, but they're not being led by fear either.

Third, I let my story lead, not just my strategy. Sometimes, I'll share a failure from earlier in my career, not to impress them, but to show that growth is part of the journey. That's how I build reliability without losing respect.

This is why it builds trust: When people see both your strength and your struggle, they realize you're not performing for them, you're leading with them. You become real. In high-stakes environments, where everyone is bracing for the next political shift, that realness becomes a safe space. Not soft. Not fragile. Grounded. Human. True. That's the kind of leader people follow into hard spaces, because they know you won't disappear behind the title when things get real.

Building Trust Under Pressure

In high-stakes environments where timelines are tight, visibility is high, and the margin for error feels razor-thin, the instinct is often to tighten control, speak less, share less, and push harder. Somewhere in that relentless grind, trust can get sidelined in favor of urgency and optics.

But here's what I've learned: the higher the pressure, the more essential trust becomes. Because under pressure, people don't just follow directions, they follow certainty, consistency, and clarity. They follow leaders they trust to carry the mission and protect the people doing the work.

The key to building trust under pressure is staying rooted while everything else moves. The stakes will shift, the politics will shift, the expectations will shift. But if you shift too much, if your tone, your presence, or your principles keep changing to match the room, you become unpredictable. And trust can't grow in uncertainty. The real key is to be the leader they can count on, not just when things are going well, but when things get real.

Here's how I build trust during high-stakes seasons:

First, I lead with calm in chaos. I don't perform confidence, I practice groundedness. When my team sees that I'm steady, even when I don't have all the answers, they breathe easier. That's leadership.

Second, I name reality and reinforce direction. I tell the truth: "This is hard. This is fast. This is complex." Whatever the scenario is, I acknowledge it. But I don't stop there. I follow it with: "Here's how we move forward together." That balance earns buy-in, because people trust leaders who can hold tension and still cast vision.

Third, I protect my people in public and push them in private. In high-pressure moments, I don't throw others under the bus to save face. I take responsibility. I shield them. Then, behind closed doors, we grow together. We recalibrate. That's the kind of leadership that builds deep loyalty.

The real test of leadership is this: Anyone can be trusted when everything is calm. But when the stakes are high, when someone's reputation is on the line, when eyes are watching, and emotions are running high, that's when trust is truly tested and either reinforced or broken. The key isn't to perform strength; it's to be consistent enough that people know exactly what version of you they'll get, even under pressure. Because when people trust that you'll show up with clarity over chaos, presence over panic, and integrity over impulse,they'll follow you anywhere.

For individuals facing high-stakes moments, I suggest reflecting on three things:

- How do you show up when the pressure hits? Are you reactive? Performative? Or grounded? Sit with that and think about specific moments where your response revealed your leadership style.
- What do people say they trust most about you? Is that trust consistent?
- How do you build and protect trust when decisions become public, personal, and political?

Creating a Culture That's Safe and Stretched

Trust is personal, but culture is collective. If trust is the foundation, then how you build on it determines whether your team survives, or scales. The next leadership challenge is this: Can you create a space where people feel safe enough to be real, yet stretched enough to grow?

Here's the tension: too much safety without challenge breeds comfort. Too much stretch without safety breeds fear. But together, safety and stretch create transformation. That's the sweet spot every high-performing, soul-centered leader must master.

What safety really means is this: Psychological safety doesn't mean avoiding hard conversations. It means people trust that telling the truth won't cost them their dignity, that they can challenge upward, fail forward, and ask questions without fear of punishment or passive retaliation. It's not about being nice; it's about being anchored in humanity.

What stretch really looks like is this: Stretch doesn't mean burnout. It means people are called higher, toward purpose, toward excellence, toward growth. It's about creating a space where standards are clear, feedback is direct, and mediocrity isn't normalized. Stretch isn't pressure; it's possibility.

There is a way to lead with both. The key isn't choosing between them, it's building the capacity to hold them in tension. That means listening deeply while still driving performance. Affirming people's value while still expecting results. Making room for process while never losing sight of purpose. Your team knows, "I can show up fully here, and I'll still be called to rise." That's not soft leadership; it's soulful accountability.

As you build trust as your foundation, reflect on these questions:

- Is my team more safe than stretched, or more stretched than safe?
- Where might I be protecting people from discomfort instead of leading them through it?
- What would it take to create a space where people feel both seen and sharpened?

Chapter 9:

Creating Cultures Of Safety And Stretch

Safety plus stretch equals soulful performance. Creating a culture where your team feels both safe and challenged means leading with both truth and trust. It means your people don't just feel protected, they feel inspired to grow. Not to prove themselves, but to become more than they thought possible. Because real leadership isn't about comfort. And it's not about chaos either. It's about building the kind of environment where people know, "I can bring my full self to work and still be called to rise."

Balancing Safety with Challenge

What safety means in practice Psychological safety isn't about coddling, it's about creating an environment where people can speak the truth without fear of backlash. Failure is seen as feedback, not a final judgment. Everyone knows their voice matters, even without a title. Culture isn't merely tolerated; it's valued as a leadership asset. Safety says: "You belong here fully."

What stretch looks like in practice

Stretch isn't about pressure; it's about purpose. It's not about raising the bar, it's about raising belief in what people are capable of. That means offering real-time, clear, and challenging feedback with care. You expect excellence because you believe in their potential. And you push people beyond their comfort zones without stripping them of their dignity. Stretch says: "You can grow here, deeply."

The cost of leading with only one if you lead only with safety, your team may love the culture but stall in performance. If you lead only with stretch, they might hit the goals, but at the cost of trust, wellness, and retention. Culture without stretch becomes comfort. Culture without safety becomes trauma.

Your job as a leader your role is to hold both safety and stretch, even when it's hard, even when your own leadership is being stretched in the process. If you can create a space where people feel seen without being shielded, heard without being coddled, and valued without being infantilized, you won't just build a high-performing team, you'll build a legacy-level culture.

That's when the real results begin, when you learn to blend both.

Human-Centered and Results-Driven

One of the biggest myths in leadership is this: you can either be a people leader or a results leader, but not both. Especially as a Black man in senior leadership, there's often a pull to over-index on one side: either becoming the empathetic fixer who carries everyone's weight, or the hyper-efficient enforcer who delivers at all costs. But I've learned the truth is far more nuanced, and far more powerful. You can lead with heart and still hold the line. You can acknowledge people's humanity and still demand excellence. You can care deeply without coddling, and push hard without dehumanizing. The key lies in how you do it.

Here are four ways to start:

1. Lead with story, not just metrics.

Results matter, but people show up differently when they feel seen beyond their tasks. I make it a point to understand what motivates my team, their context, and what's happening beyond the performance dashboard. That doesn't mean I lower the bar, it means I lead from relationship, not just responsibility. When you know your people's story, you lead with nuance, not assumptions.

2. Set standards through values, not just deadlines.

I don't just say, "Get it done because I said so." I say, "We deliver with excellence because we represent something bigger than ourselves." I root expectations in culture, legacy, and shared identity. That way, the pressure isn't just external, it becomes personal, purposeful, and collective. That's when the shift happens, from "we have to" to "we get to." And that's when synergy starts to build.

3. Give feedback that sharpens without shaming.

I don't sugarcoat feedback, but I never deliver it like a weapon. I might say, "I believe in your potential, and here's where we're not hitting it yet." Or, "This doesn't align with the excellence I know you're capable of." Or, "I care too much about your growth to let this slide." Then I deliver the feedback. That way, people feel challenged and supported at the same time.

4. Hold space without lowering the bar.

Life happens. Burnout is real. People hit walls. But instead of saying, "Don't worry about it," I might say, "Let's reset the plan, but not the purpose." Or, "Let's pause the pace, but not the standard." Or even, "Let's shift the support, but not the expectation." Holding space isn't about lowering standards, it's about being flexible without being fuzzy.

Ultimately, your people should walk away from your leadership feeling two things: He sees me. And, He won't let me settle. That's how you lead with both dignity and demand. That's how you build trust that performs. That's how you create stretch that doesn't snap.

Authenticity as a Performance Driver

Being authentic doesn't mean being soft. It doesn't mean saying whatever comes to mind in the moment, and it certainly doesn't mean unpacking your trauma in every team meeting to seem relatable. Authenticity in leadership means leading from alignment, not from a need for approval. It means your words, values, and decisions are rooted in who you are, not in the rooms you're trying to access.

This matters because when you lead from that place, you stop managing perception and start mobilizing trust. And trust real trust is the bedrock of high performance.

What authentic leadership unlocks in a team comes down to three things:

First, psychological safety, which fuels risk-taking. When your team sees you leading from trust, steadiness, and humility, they stop tiptoeing. They start taking initiative. They speak up. They innovate without waiting for perfect conditions. That's how cultures shift from passive to powerful.

Second, emotional buy-in, which ultimately leads to greater ownership. Authenticity builds connection, and connection builds loyalty. When people believe in you, they care more about what they're building with you. They don't just meet the standard, they protect the mission.

Third, cultural permission, which translates to full participation. When you lead with your whole self, you give others unspoken permission to stop code-switching, shape-shifting, and shrinking. The room becomes sharper. Smarter. Braver. Why? Because people are contributing from identity, not just from their job description.

My leadership shift: There was a time I tried to lead like those who came before me, polished, distant, and calculated. And while the results were there, the team wasn't thriving. Deliverables were tight, but the culture felt tense. People said the right things, but trust was surface-level.

So I made a shift. I started naming hard things. I began showing more of how I think, not just what I expect. I led from story, not just strategy. And what happened? Performance didn't drop. It deepened. It sharpened. It became more resilient. Because people don't perform at their best when they're being watched. They perform at their best when they're seen.

Authentic leadership requires clarity of values, knowing what you stand for before the room puts you to the test. It demands emotional discipline: sharing vulnerably without oversharing. It calls for cultural intelligence, creating space for difference without lowering the bar. And it depends on consistency of presence: not disappearing when pressure mounts.

Authenticity is something people feel. When they do, they follow it, trust it, and perform for it, not out of fear, but from a place of shared belief.

When I coach leaders stepping into this mindset, I challenge them to reflect on three core questions:

- Where in my leadership am I hiding or hardening under the guise of professionalism?
- What might shift if I led with truth and trusted that alignment fuels performance?
- How am I modeling authenticity in ways that invite rather than intimidate my team?

Empathy as Leadership Intelligence

Empathy is not a weakness. It's not passive. It's not coddling. And it's definitely not just about being nice. Empathy is intelligence. Empathy is strategy. Empathy is leadership. When you're leading a team under pressure, navigating change, or chasing big goals, empathy is what helps you read the room without losing sight of the mission.

Empathy is the bridge between support and stretch. For Black men elevated into senior leadership, you're expected to perform, to lead, and often, to do it with zero margin for error. So, empathy might feel risky. It might feel vulnerable, even unprofessional, in certain spaces.

106

But here's what I've learned: empathy is what separates leaders who merely manage people from those who mobilize potential.

When you lead with empathy, you don't just react to numbers; you respond to nuance. You don't just push harder; you check if the foundation is strong enough to hold the weight. You don't just deliver outcomes; you develop people. Empathy drives high performance.

How? By giving you the context to lead well. You ask extra questions. You see the person behind the performance. And that insight lets you stretch people without snapping them. Empathy builds emotional trust before the challenge even hits. When people know you see them as more than what they produce, they don't resist feedback, they lean into it. They know it's coming from belief, not just demand.

Empathy turns pressure into partnership. Instead of saying, "Figure it out," you say, "Here's what I expect, and here's how I'll support you in getting there." It's not you versus them; it's you with them.

How I use empathy in senior leadership spaces: When a deadline slips or performance dips, I don't just ask what happened, I ask what shifted, what got in the way, what's the story underneath the slip. Empathy doesn't mean lowering expectations. It means understanding how to help people reach them.

Sometimes I challenge with directness. Sometimes I pause and recalibrate, based on what someone is carrying. But every time, I lead with humanity and accountability. That balance makes me a better leader. It makes us a better team. It creates a culture that performs without pretending.

Derrick, a senior VP of strategy and operations at a global tech firm, once told me:

"I used to lead with edge alone. But when I brought empathy into the mix, people stopped fearing me and started following me. Now I get performance and loyalty, because they know I don't just see results. I see them."

It's so important to bridge the gap between results and people. And to do that, you have to lead with empathy.

When The Leader Burns Out

You can build the most affirming culture. You can stretch others with empathy and lead from alignment. But none of that matters if you're leading on empty. Because the truth is, even the strongest leaders burn out, especially when you're a Black man holding space for everyone else.

For years, I believed leadership meant carrying it all. I thought it meant keeping the team going, delivering outcomes, staying sharp, smiling through the pain, and pushing forward when tired. And if nobody noticed what it cost? That was just part of the job, right?

But that mindset is a slow death. Burnout doesn't begin with exhaustion; it begins with disconnection, from your voice, your body, and the purpose that once lit you up. You start leading from survival. You start making decisions from depletion. And eventually, the leader becomes the one most in need of saving.

How I navigated burnout: I hit a wall that success couldn't fix. The title didn't protect me. The strategy didn't refill me. I had built strong teams, but I ignored my own humanity. Here's what I realized:

You can't build sustainable culture if your soul is quietly unraveling. So I stopped pretending. I started listening to the tension in my body. I began naming what I was carrying, not just professionally, but emotionally. I took off the mask. First with myself, then with people I trusted. And most importantly, I stopped wearing resilience as a badge. I began treating restoration as a leadership strategy.

Burnout taught me this: You don't have to break to take a break. Rest is not a reward for performance, it's a prerequisite for purpose. You can lead boldly and still protect your peace. Burnout isn't a weakness; it's a signal. And if you listen early, it doesn't have to mark the end of your leadership, it can reshape it. Because when you return from burnout with clarity, boundaries, and alignment, you don't just survive the system. You lead in a way that transforms it.

For leaders wondering if they're in burnout, approaching burnout, or ready to move past it, I invite them to reflect on three questions:

- First, where am I ignoring the signs of burnout because I'm afraid to slow down?
- Second, who have I built safety for, and have I built it for myself?
- Third, what would it look like to reset my leadership without retreating from it?

When you really sit with those questions, you'll begin to assess where you are in the burnout process. And just remember: burnout can be reshaped.

PART 4:

FROM STRUGGLE TO STRATEGY

Chapter 10:

What Burnout Taught Me

Burnout didn't just hit me, it hollowed me out. It wasn't a dramatic collapse at my desk or an emotional outburst in a meeting. It was slower, quieter, and more dangerous because of it. It looked like showing up to lead a meeting and feeling nothing. It looked like delivering results while feeling completely disconnected from the why. It sounded like saying "I'm good" while silently wondering if I still believed in what I was building. It meant looking successful on the outside and feeling erased on the inside.

That's the part people don't talk about. Burnout is often invisible, especially among high-performing, high-stakes leaders, because performance becomes the mask. And for Black men in leadership, that mask becomes armor. We're taught to wear it, rewarded for carrying the weight, and expected to never let it show.

The Silent Lessons of Burnout

Burnout taught me three things. First, survival mode is not leadership. I was leading out of muscle memory, showing up because I knew how to show up. But I wasn't truly present. I wasn't whole. And I realized: you can't lead people into freedom if you're bound yourself.

Second, boundaries are not optional; they're oxygen. I had been saying yes out of obligation, taking meetings I didn't believe in, protecting others while neglecting my own peace. Burnout taught me that everything costs something. The only question is: who pays? Now, I build boundaries that reflect my capacity, not just my character, as I move forward in leadership.

Third, identity can't be built on performance alone. When I couldn't deliver at the same level, I began to question my worth. That's when it hit me: I had tied my identity to outcomes. Burnout stripped that away. What was left was just me, the real me. The one I had to relearn how to care for, to listen to, and to lead from.

The turning point: One day, I sat in a parking lot after a major win, a successful launch, glowing feedback from the C-suite. My team was proud. And I felt nothing. Not joy, not fulfillment, not even relief. That was a wake-up call. Because if the win doesn't fill you, if the applause doesn't ground you, if the grind is no longer connected to your purpose, you're not leading. You're leaking.

What I lead with now: I rest before I'm forced to. I lead from rhythm, not rescue. I check in with myself as much as I check in on my team. I no longer believe in choosing between impact and well-being. I lead from both. Burnout doesn't have to end your leadership; it can redefine it. Now, I lead from a place of fullness, not just function.

For those wrestling with burnout, I encourage reflection on these questions:

- Where has burnout shown up as numbness, over-functioning, or quiet resentment?
- What leadership rhythms have I normalized that are actually draining me?
- What would change if I started leading from wholeness, not just output?

The Burnout Recovery Map (Monthly Leadership Tool)

This tool guides you through the four essential zones of burnout recovery: awareness, boundaries, restoration, and alignment. Use it as a map to identify where you are, acknowledge what's true, and navigate your way back to full, unapologetic leadership.

Zone 1: Awareness, Spot the Symptoms

Burnout often wears the mask of high performance. Recognize the signs before they silence you.

Check any that apply:

☐ You're delivering results but feel disconnected from your deeper purpose.

☐ You're avoiding crucial conversations because there's nothing left in the tank.

☐ You feel resentment toward roles or responsibilities that once inspired you.

☐ Rest feels like a luxury, not a leadership necessity.

☐ You're consistently exhausted, even after a full night's sleep.

☐ You're present for everyone else but absent for yourself.

Journal Prompt:

Where am I most depleted, and what truth have I been avoiding about it?

Zone 2: Boundaries – Protect the Essentials

Every "yes" comes at a cost. What have you been giving away without refilling your own cup?

Reflection Questions

- What am I saying "yes" to that no longer supports my well-being or aligns with my mission?

- Where am I overextending myself just to stay visible, liked, or needed?

- Which boundaries, whether time, emotional, digital, or energetic, have I neglected to uphold?

Write 3 New Boundaries

I will no longer _____

I will only accept _____

I will protect my energy by _____

Zone 3: Restoration – Reclaim Rhythm

You don't restore by stopping everything. You restore by returning to what fills you.

Choose three practices to help restore your leadership rhythm:

- Silence – Take daily unplugged time (no screens, just stillness).
- Movement – Engage in walks, workouts, yoga, or stretching.
- Reflection – Journal, pray, attend therapy, or practice spirituality.
- Joy – Immerse yourself in music, laughter, hobbies, art, or nature.
- Connection – Spend time with mentors, soul-friends, or in non-work conversations.

Journal Prompt:

When do I feel most grounded, most creative, or most fully myself?

How can I make that feeling non-negotiable again?

Zone 4: Alignment – Redefine the Mission

Burnout forces you to ask: Am I performing leadership, or truly living it?

Take a moment to reflect and craft your Leadership Alignment Statement, a new declaration of how you will lead from this point forward.

My Leadership Alignment Statement:

- "I will lead from conviction, not obligation."
- "My peace is not the price of my performance."
- "I will no longer sacrifice my well-being for external validation."

Final Commitment:

What is one intentional action I will take this week to honor my recovery and realign with my purpose?

This week, I will schedule daily quiet time, even just 15 minutes, to reconnect with my inner clarity and restore my energy.

REVISIT THIS MAP MONTHLY:

Because burnout doesn't always crash in, it creeps in. Revisit this tool to stay honest, stay grounded, and stay aligned with what truly matters.

Burnout doesn't mean you're broken. It means it's time to rebuild, with clarity, boundaries, and the deep belief that your wholeness matters more than your output.

Resetting Without Retreating

Burnout will tempt you to walk away from everything, your mission, your influence, your own voice. But I knew I couldn't disappear. Too much was at stake. Too many people were watching. And most of all, I still believed in the work. So I had to ask myself:

- "How do I reset without retreating?"
- "How do I protect my peace without compromising my power?"

The answer wasn't a dramatic exit. It was a disciplined return to myself. I did that in four steps.

Step One: I got ruthlessly clear on what was draining me. I didn't just name the exhaustion, I tracked the sources. I asked: Where am I overextending out of guilt? Where am I showing up for others in ways I'm not showing up for myself? What meetings, dynamics, even relationships are depleting me? I mapped it out line by line, because you can't reset what you won't own.

Step Two: I redrew my boundaries, out loud. I didn't just say I needed more balance. I communicated clear, non-negotiable boundaries around my time, energy, and focus. And I stated them with confidence, not apology. For example: "I won't be responding to messages after 6 p.m.", and I modeled that for my team.

I said things like: *"I'm stepping back from non-mission-critical meetings this quarter to protect strategic capacity," or "I'm not available to process issues that belong to HR, therapy, or someone else in that chain of command."* Because boundaries don't limit your leadership, they legitimize it.

Step Three: I invited support without releasing responsibility. I wasn't looking to be rescued, but I was done pretending I didn't need help. I leaned into my executive coach. I checked in with my mentors. I told my team I was recalibrating, and gave them permission to do the same. That was vulnerability. But it wasn't weakness, it was strategy. The result? More loyalty, more buy-in, more human momentum.

Step Four: I recommitted to leading from rhythm, not reaction. Before burnout, I was always responding to whatever came at me. After burnout, I moved differently. I started blocking time for deep work and deep rest. I built recovery space into my calendar, not just recovery language into my leadership. I stopped using crisis as a leadership style. I re-centered clarity as my compass. That rhythm made me more decisive, not less. More respected, not less. Because now I wasn't just leading from muscle, I was leading from alignment.

"When I finally stopped pretending I was fine and started recalibrating how I lead, the people who mattered didn't see it as retreat. They saw it as maturity. Resetting saved my leadership before the job could take it from me."

Andre, Chief Legal Officer, Fortune 500 Fintech

The lesson? Resetting isn't stepping back, it's stepping into your leadership differently. It allows you to preserve your purpose without bleeding through your performance. It rebuilds credibility through consistency, not hyper-productivity. You stay at the table without losing your soul on the way there. Because rest doesn't make you less effective, it makes you whole enough to lead what's next.

Reflection Prompts for the Reader:

- What would a true reset look like, not a vacation, but a leadership recalibration?
- What boundary or rhythm do I need to re-establish this week?
- Who can I invite into my recovery plan without giving up my responsibility?

Building a Sustainable Leadership Practice

If your leadership is thriving but your spirit is crumbling, that's not success, it's survival in disguise. As Black men in high-profile roles, we're often applauded for what we carry but rarely asked how it's carrying us. The pressure to deliver, to protect, to represent, to never break, it wears on the mind, the body, the spirit. If you don't build a system that nourishes you, leadership will quietly, completely drain you.

I had to learn: success without soul is not sustainable. Grind without grace will grind you into the ground. So how do I manage this balance, mentally, emotionally, and spiritually? First, I honor my humanity. Not last, first. I stopped viewing rest, therapy, spiritual check-ins, and boundaries as recovery tools and started treating them as leadership infrastructure. I wake up and align before I perform. I check how I'm feeling before I check emails. Because if I don't center myself, the world will center me around urgency, noise, and ego.

Second, I protect my mental health like an executive assistant. I block white space in my calendar, not just for work, but for mental breathing room. Too often, we're in spaces with back-to-back meetings and no time to actually breathe. I keep a coach and a therapist on rotation, not because I'm broken, but because I'm responsible. I journal when I'm clear and when I'm confused, because reflection gives me distance from emotional hijack.

Third, I guard my emotional energy like it's sacred. Not every conversation deserves me. Not every conflict requires my emotional labor. I've learned to stop absorbing dysfunction and start naming where my energy ends and the system begins. Sometimes, leadership is about discernment: I see the fire, but I won't bring my peace into it unless I'm called to extinguish it.

Fourth, I maintain a spiritual rhythm, not just a religious routine. I don't just pray when I'm unwell; I pray so I don't break. I don't only reflect on Sundays; I live in reflection.

I keep a circle of people who ask me soul-level questions like:

- "Are you leading from conviction or coping?"
- "Is your pace still aligned with your purpose?"
- "Where's your joy hiding right now?"

Questions like these help me stay connected to my internal self. My spiritual life isn't separate from my leadership, it is the leadership.

The non-negotiable is this: stop making self-protection optional. The higher you rise, the more intentional you must be about staying anchored. Because when people expect you to be the answer, you have to remember, you're not the source. You're the vessel, and the vessel must stay full.

So, I stopped glorifying the grind. I stopped letting busyness define my self-worth. I began leading from a place of overflow, not obligation.

Malik, a regional director in healthcare operations, once said to me,

"You can't hold the weight of a system if your soul isn't rooted in something deeper than that system.

I stopped trying to be the strong Black executive and started being the whole one. That's when I found peace. I didn't have to earn it."

As individuals at this inflection point, it's important to ask ourselves:

- What daily rhythms keep you anchored, mentally, emotionally, and spiritually?
- What needs to be added or removed so you stop managing your breakdown and start protecting your balance?

- Who helps you stay human, not just high-performing?

A Message to Brothers on the Brink

To the brother on the brink, let me talk to you directly.If you're reading this and feeling the weight, the quiet kind, the one that doesn't show up in an HR report but lives in your chest, your spirit, and your silence, I need you to hear this:

You are not weak for feeling tired. You are not broken for wanting to pause. You are not alone for wondering, "How long can I carry this?" This is the cost no one talks about. Leadership will praise you for being the strongest, for always showing up, for never missing a beat, until one day, you can't hear the beat anymore because the pressure has drowned out the purpose.

So here's my advice, heart to heart, leader to leader:

First, stop waiting for the collapse to justify the rest. You don't need a breakdown to deserve a break. You don't need to flatline before you hit pause. Rest doesn't have to be reactive, make it revolutionary. Start treating rest like a strategy, not just recovery.

Second, say what's draining you, out loud. We don't talk about it enough. Burnout thrives in silence. If you're carrying too much in your head or on your heart, speak it, to the mirror, to your circle, to your coach. Because what you won't name will quietly own you.

Third, reclaim your rhythm before the system sets your pace.

This world will have you sprinting toward burnout and calling it purpose. So slow down. Reset your morning. Rewrite your week. Don't just manage time, protect your energy.

Fourth, don't confuse performance with presence. You've done enough performing. Now start showing up as the whole version of you, not just the version they reward. Because presence isn't loud, but it's anchored.

Fifth, ask for help before you convince yourself you don't need it. We've been conditioned to carry the load alone, but isolation is not strength, it's a setup. Find your people. Hire your help. Drop the shame. Leadership is shared, even when the title suggests otherwise.

And most of all, remember this: You are not just your output. You are not just a provider, a fixer, or a voice in the room. You are a whole human being. Your leadership does not require your depletion to be valid. Take a pause. Reset the rhythm. And remember: you can lead powerfully and protect your peace. That's not weakness. That's wisdom.

Evan, an executive coach and former Chief Operating Officer in the education space, once said to me during a coaching session,

"The best decision I made wasn't a promotion. It was pulling back before I broke down. That pause gave me breath. That breath brought me back to myself. And that version of me, he's the one I trust now."

As a final reflection for those in this space, ask yourself three questions:

- What are my body, spirit, and silence trying to tell me?
- What does my leadership need less of right now, and what does it need more of?
- What am I willing to protect, even if no one applauds it along the way?

Reclaiming Your Voice After Burnout

The comeback wasn't loud, it was aligned. Burnout didn't just take my energy; it chipped away at my voice, that inner clarity, that unapologetic tone I once led with. It didn't shrink my space physically, but emotionally. I found myself asking for permission to speak, overthinking everything, choosing silence over truth just to preserve a peace I hadn't even protected for myself.

But here's the shift I made: I didn't fight to get my old voice back. I fought to find my true one, the voice not rooted in performance, the one that didn't rise and fall with other people's reactions. The one that had always been there, buried beneath expectation, pace, and pain.

I went through a process of reclaiming my voice. I stopped editing my tone to sound less intense. I started speaking from alignment. I began trusting my instincts again, not just the metrics or the mood in the room. I said no more often, and I didn't explain it in a paragraph. The more I honored my internal voice, the less I sought external permission.

How I reclaimed my space: I started taking up space, not through volume, but through presence. I stopped shrinking my leadership style to fit into rooms too small for my calling. I redesigned my calendar, my relationships, and my recovery time to reflect my worth, not just my role. Because space isn't something the system hands you; it's something you claim when you stop apologizing for your power.

The lesson is: burnout didn't make me disappear. It made me reintroduce myself, this time, fully. When I came back, I didn't just lead the work. I led differently, louder in conviction, quieter in performance, stronger in boundaries, and softer in ego. I wasn't just back; I was rooted.

Some of the reflections I went through, and encourage other leaders to explore, include:

- Where have I lost my voice, not just from silence, but from self-protection?
- What space am I shrinking, that I actually need to own?
- What version of me is trying to emerge on the other side of this burnout?

Chapter 11:

Owning Your Voice, Owning Your Space

You can't dismantle a system you're too afraid to challenge. I've sat at tables where speaking up felt like lighting a match in a room soaked with gasoline, where telling the truth carried a silent cost: the raised eyebrows, the "circle back" meetings that happened without me, the gradual exclusion from rooms I helped build. And still, I chose to speak. Not out of rage. Not recklessly. I spoke with rootedness, from strategy, from clarity, from alignment with something deeper than ego.

What I learned is this: you don't win by staying silent. You don't win by being reckless either. You win by being undeniably aligned.

Strategic Disruption Without Self-Destruction

How I challenged the system without becoming its casualty was by refusing to lead from emotion alone. I began speaking from strategy. The system is designed to label your emotions as aggressive, so when I pushed back, I made sure I was clear, not just right. I named patterns, not just moments. I framed my words around values, mission, and risk, not just frustration. And I brought receipts, because truth without proof is too easily dismissed as opinion.

I used my voice like a scalpel, not a sledgehammer. I learned to say less, but say it sharper. Sometimes, one sentence in the right room moves more than a whole speech in the wrong one. I asked questions that made the room uncomfortable, without making myself disposable. Questions like: "What are we communicating if the only leaders promoted don't reflect the people doing the work?" Or: "How do we define excellence, and who created that definition?" I aimed for the root of the issue, without uprooting myself in the process. I built quiet power before I took public stands. I didn't just show up and demand change, I earned trust. I studied patterns. I moved relationally. So when I challenged the system, I wasn't speaking into the room; I was speaking from within it. That gave my words weight.

I defined my line, and I didn't apologize for it. There are hills you die on and hills you build strategy on. I learned to know the difference. I made peace with this: If I lose access by standing in truth, it was never access, it was control. What that taught me is this: you can challenge the system and keep your soul. You can speak truth without losing your seat, but only if you stop performing and start positioning. Because the system doesn't just fear your voice; it fears your clarity.

Your Story is Your Strategy

For a long time, I led like I was writing someone else's script, polished, predictable, professional. Just enough personality to seem relatable, but never enough to fully know me or for me to fully be myself. What I learned was this: when you don't lead from your own story, you end up living out someone else's agenda. You become the safe Black leader. The translator. The face on the DEI flyer. Over time, your presence feels performative, even to you.

So I started leading from a different place. I started telling the truth, not just the facts. I started leading from story. And that changed everything. When I think about how story helped me reclaim my space, the first thing it did was humanize my leadership. When I shared parts of my journey, what I overcame, what shaped my leadership values, people stopped seeing me as just a role and started seeing me as real. I created connections without code-switching. It reminded them, and myself, that I wasn't just here because I could deliver outcomes. I was here because I have a lived perspective that adds depth to the strategy.

Story disrupted the room, without exploding it. Instead of arguing data or fighting politics, I shared narratives that reframed the issue. Like the time I talked about watching brilliant team members get passed over, not because of performance, but because their presence made people uncomfortable. I said, "We say we value equity, but I've watched it get filtered through comfort. And when equity has to pass through comfort, we lose talent that looks like me."

That hit differently. The conversation shifted, not because I got louder, but because the story made it undeniable. The more I told my story, how I led, why I led, what I no longer tolerate, the less I needed the system to define me.

I don't need to be the person you respect, I can be who I am and still lead at the highest level. Story became my anchor, not for attention, but for authority. Not to explain myself, but to stand firm in what I know.

"Once I started telling my story in rooms where I was only known through performance, everything changed. I wasn't just tolerated, I was trusted. People connect with story more than they connect with stats."

Julian, Senior Director, Government Relations & Public Policy

Storytelling is powerful for Black men because the system wasn't built for your voice, it was built for your silence. It was built to flatten you into "the one who made it." Your story pushes back against that flattening. Your story says: "I came through systems that weren't made for me." Your story says: "I lead differently because I carry wisdom not learned in the boardroom." Your story says: "I don't have to perform pain for you, but I will lead from what shaped me."

That's not emotionalism. That's executive clarity, rooted in lived experience.

I often encourage people to reflect on:

- Where have I stayed quiet about my story to remain comfortable or avoid tension?
- What moment in my journey could unlock understanding, alignment, or change?
- How can I use storytelling as a leadership strategy this week, not just a personal detail?

Voice + Space Power Map Tool:

Your leadership doesn't just need volume, it needs visibility. It needs voice. And it needs space you don't apologize for.

This tool helps you assess where your leadership voice is being used with power, and where your presence is being minimized, sidelined, or stretched out of alignment.

It's divided into three zones:

- Where your voice is strong
- Where your space is shrinking
- Where you need to reclaim power

ZONE 1: Where Is My Voice Strong?

This is where your influence is honored, your tone is trusted, and your perspective shifts the room.

Reflection Questions:

- Which spaces (teams, rooms, relationships) consistently receive my leadership with weight and clarity?
- Where am I listened to without needing to perform?
- Where do I feel most aligned in how I speak, lead, and decide?

Examples:

- Executive team strategy calls
- 1:1s with direct reports
- Leading during crisis or ambiguity

Anchor Statement:

"In these spaces, I speak with clarity and am heard with respect."

ZONE 2: Where Is My Space Being Minimized?

This is where your presence is tolerated but not trusted, or where you shrink yourself to stay safe.

Reflection Questions:

- Where do I feel I have to over-explain, soften, or code-switch to be taken seriously?
- Where am I consistently interrupted, ignored, or reinterpreted?

- What meetings, roles, or interactions make me feel like I'm performing leadership rather than living it?

Examples:

- Cross-functional meetings where my expertise is questioned
- Conversations where decisions are made before I'm invited
- Roles where I'm the "only" and expected to serve as a cultural consultant

Anchor Statement:

"In these spaces, I'm shrinking or surviving, not leading."

ZONE 3: Where Do I Need to Reclaim Power?

This is where you must reestablish your leadership presence, with intention, strategy, and conviction.

Action Questions:

- What specific space, person, or structure do I need to engage differently?
- Where do I need to say less, with more clarity, or speak up where I've gone silent?
- Where have I been playing small to avoid being labeled as too "aggressive," "opinionated," or "difficult"?

My Reclamation Commitments:

I will name _____ with clear language and strategic timing.

I will stop softening _____ to make others comfortable.

I will reclaim space in _____ by showing up with

_____.

Use This Tool Monthly

Revisit this map each quarter or during major transitions. Your leadership voice will continue to evolve, and the system will continue to test it.

But with clarity comes power.

And with power comes presence.

The kind they can't dismiss. The kind you no longer dilute.

Standing Ground with Strategy, Not Just Strength

Standing your ground isn't about making noise; it's about knowing. Resistance will come, no matter where you are in your leadership journey. When you begin leading from your own voice instead of their comfort, the system will push back. When you stop explaining your presence and start owning it, people will feel uncomfortable, not because you're wrong, but because you're no longer playing the role they assigned you.

So when resistance showed up, dismissive comments, subtle retaliation, coded feedback, or the classic "You're not being a team player" rhetoric, I had a choice: shrink back and survive or stand my ground and lead. I chose the latter, not recklessly, but strategically.

First, I clarified my non-negotiables before the conflict. I didn't wait until I was in the fire to figure out where I stood. I wrote down what I would not compromise. I listed the treatment, dynamics, and behaviors I would not tolerate. I identified the parts of my voice and identity that were non-negotiable. So when the pressure came, I wasn't confused. You don't rise to the occasion; you fall to the level of your preparation.

Second, I led with calm, not emotion. Most people expect fire; I chose to bring clarity. I didn't yell to be heard. I spoke like someone who knew the room wasn't ready, but would listen anyway. Whether I was challenging a decision, naming a bias, or holding a boundary, I slowed my delivery and sharpened my message. Because when your tone is steady, they have to focus on your content, not your expression.

I also positioned my conviction in the language of strategy. I stopped arguing from personal frustration and started speaking in terms of business risk, cultural alignment, brand impact, and long-term performance. For example: "If we continue overlooking diverse voices in strategy conversations, the blind spots won't just affect morale, they'll affect market relevance." That's not just passion, that's strategic positioning.

I made peace with what resistance might cost me. This is a hard truth: every time you stand your ground, something may shift. You may be excluded from conversations. You might not be liked. You could lose proximity to certain power circles. But what you won't lose is your self-respect, your alignment, your voice. And when your leadership is rooted in purpose, not just permission, you can stand in the tension without breaking.

What ultimately sustained me was building power outside the system. I didn't rely on a single organization to define or affirm me. I mentored. I coached. I spoke. I created. So when resistance came, I had a leadership identity that wasn't tied to the approval of one room. That's how you protect your voice from becoming fragile.

I encourage people to reflect on these three questions:

- Where have you been softening the truth to avoid resistance?
- What are the three non-negotiables you need to reaffirm in your leadership?
- What power are you building outside the rooms that merely tolerate you?

Challenging the Blueprint That Wasn't Built for Us

You don't just disrupt the system you've been disappearing into. There's a blueprint for how to "make it" in leadership, and that blueprint wasn't written with us in mind. The deeper you go, the more pressure there is to assimilate, to smooth your edges, to become "strategic" which is often just code for silence.

But here's what I know as a Black man in leadership: if you challenge the system by becoming the system, all you've really done is renovate a house that still doesn't belong to you. So I had to make a decision. I wasn't going to succeed in the system, I was going to lead in a way that shifts it. To do that, I had to stay authentic, not performative. I challenged systemic barriers on my own terms. I did that by naming what others avoided, but with strategic precision. I didn't just rant about equity. I brought data, stories, and language the system had to respect. I framed my truth in ways that exposed bias without making myself a target. I called things what they were, but with tact and timing.

For example: "This policy disproportionately affects our emerging Black talent, and if we don't shift it, we're not just losing employees, we're losing future leaders." That's not just critique; that's strategic disruption.

Second, I refused to lead from a script that wasn't mine. I stopped trying to sound like the executives before me. I brought my own tone, my clarity, my lived lens, and I let my results speak for my approach. Because authenticity without impact is noise. But authenticity with performance? That's undeniable. I knew that if I wanted to shift the system, I had to model another way to lead. We often talk about soft skills, external things we can do to move toward leadership, but we rarely discuss the internal mindsets that get us there. For me, it's crucial to be able to look in the mirror and genuinely say: I'm still myself.

One way I did that was by holding the line when things got uncomfortable. When asked to co-sign on performative DEI efforts, I said no. When invited to advise but not decide, I renegotiated my role, or walked away. I didn't fight every battle, but I chose the right ones and showed up fully. Authenticity means being able to look myself in the mirror after every meeting, not just checking off metrics.

I built coalitions, not just critiques. I challenged systems with people, not just at them. I brought in allies and elevated other Black voices. I mentored across levels, because if you want to dismantle a system, you'd better be building something new while breaking the old. Authenticity without collaboration becomes isolation. Authenticity with community creates momentum.

This matters for Black men in leadership because the system often wants your output, but not your origin. It welcomes your labor, but not your language. It rewards what you deliver, while gradually draining who you are. So the only way to stay whole is to challenge the system in ways that don't require you to become invisible within it. Authenticity doesn't mean saying everything, it means never saying what you don't believe.

Leadership as Legacy

Legacy is bigger than the room you're in. The deeper I've gone in leadership, the clearer that truth becomes. This isn't just about where I show up, it's about what I leave behind. Owning your voice and space isn't just about being heard in the moment; it's about creating blueprints, not just breakthroughs. It's about ensuring that the next Black leader doesn't have to wear a mask to be respected or shrink their soul to succeed. Because if you lead well but the system still swallows the next one, then you didn't finish the assignment.

Legacy isn't just about who remembers you; it's about what lives on after you're gone. That's why I chose to play the long game. I stopped chasing approval when I realized I'm not here to be liked, I'm here to lead in a way that leaves a lasting assignment in my wake. That's why I build teams that can thrive without me. I mentor not just for the next position, but for the next era. I document what I know. I teach what I've lived. I speak the truth, even if it makes the room tense, because comfort doesn't create change.

I'm not leading for this quarter's numbers; I'm leading for my lineage. I'm leading for the ones watching who haven't even arrived yet. So what does it mean to lead with legacy?
It means I ask deeper questions:

- What kind of culture will outlive my presence?
- What story will they tell about how I moved?
- Who got free because I stood firm?
- What systems cracked because I stopped playing small?

It's not about being perfect, it's about being intentional. Because legacy isn't built in your title. It's built in your decisions, your discipline, and your daily clarity. That's what truly matters.

So I encourage every leader to reflect on the following:

- What will my leadership make possible that wasn't possible before?

- Where am I still chasing moments, when I should be building a movement?
- What does it mean for me to lead like someone is watching who will inherit what I build?

Chapter 12:

The Long Game Of Leadership

The long game isn't about promotion, it's about preservation. When I was younger in my leadership journey, I believed playing the long game meant climbing the ladder without slipping. I thought it was all about patience, positioning, and eventually getting my name on the door. But what I've come to realize is that the long game isn't about titles, it's about timeliness. It's not about staying relevant; it's about staying rooted in something that endures, when the applause fades, when the access shifts, and when the politics change.

Legacy Over Likes: Building Beyond the Moment

What the long game means to me as a Black man in leadership comes down to three specific things.

First, it means building beyond the moment. I'm not leading just to make a quarterly impact, I'm leading so that someone coming after me won't have to fight the same battles without a blueprint. It's legacy over likes. It's system change over short-term gain. It's roots over reach.

Second, it means being strategic about what I say yes and no to. The long game forces me to ask three questions: Does this decision build the culture I want others to inherit? Will this move make me visible but disconnected from myself? Is this opportunity aligned with where I'm going, or just a distraction that feels good in the moment? I don't chase optics anymore; I chase alignment with impact.

Third, it means mentoring and coaching like my life depends on it, because if I climb the mountain alone and leave no map, I've failed. The long game is about creating capacity, not just consuming it. It's about pouring into Black men who are tired of bleeding in silence, not as a savior, but as a mirror.

The long game demands that I stay whole, because nothing sustainable is built from burnout. It's taught me to slow down, protect my peace, and lead from restoration, not ego. It's not a sprint. I'm not competing; I'm curating a life, a body of work, and a model of leadership that doesn't self-destruct at the top.

Playing the long game means I'm not just thinking about this role, this team, or this organization, I'm thinking about who I'm becoming and who gets free because I keep showing up. It's about what still stands, even when I'm gone. The long game isn't about making noise; it's about leaving a mark that outlives you.

Legacy Leadership Map:

Your real résumé isn't what you've done, it's what you've made possible.

This map invites you to step back from the day-to-day grind and ask:

"What am I truly building through my leadership, beyond the role, beyond the title?"

It's intentionally structured in four layers:

- The Foundation – Who You Are
- The Blueprint – What You Believe
- The Structure – What You're Building
- The Inheritance – What Will Outlive You?

1. The Foundation: Who Are You, Really?

Before building a legacy, you get to lead from identity, not impression.

Reflection Prompts:

- What are three non-negotiable values in how I lead?
- When I'm leading at my best, what part of me feels most alive?
- What personal story shapes my leadership, not to impress, but to align?

Anchor Statement:

"I lead from my core, not from the room's expectations."

2. The Blueprint: What Do You Believe?

Legacy isn't driven by effort alone, it's fueled by clarity.

Reflection Prompts:

- What do I believe about power, equity, voice, and visibility?
- What broken patterns do I feel called to disrupt or redesign in leadership?
- What false belief about leadership did I need to unlearn?

Blueprint Declaration:

"I believe leadership is not about climbing , it's about clearing the path for others."

3. The Structure: What Are You Building?

This is where the daily grind transforms into generational impact.

Reflection Prompts:

- What am I actively building that could outlive this organization?
- Who am I intentionally mentoring, multiplying, or molding?
- How does my leadership change because I know others are watching?

Structure Mapping:

☐ Team Culture I've Shaped: _____

☐ Systems I've Disrupted or Improved: _____

☐ Emerging Leaders I've Elevated: _____

☐ Spaces Where I've Shifted Narrative:_____

Anchor Statement:

"I'm not building for likes — I'm building for legacy."

4. The Inheritance: What Will They Carry When I'm Gone?

The final question of leadership isn't "Did I win?" it's "What did I leave behind?"

Reflection Prompts:

- What habits, rhythms, or truths will others carry because they watched me lead?
- What parts of the culture will still sound or feel like me after I've moved on?
- If they inherit my mindset, not just my wins, what will they gain?

Legacy Vision Statement:

"I want to be remembered as the leader who _____, not just the one who _____."

REVISIT THIS MAP QUARTERLY.

Legacy isn't one decision, it's a series of daily deposits. Use this map to stay aligned with what matters most, especially when the pressure says, "Perform." This is your compass. This is your anchor. This is your why, expressed in your own language.

"If leadership is about legacy, then every meeting, every boundary, and every decision is a brick laid in the foundation of something that will outlive you."

What Will They Say When You're Gone?

Legacy is the story they tell when you're no longer in the room. For me, legacy isn't a speech they give when I retire. It's not a plaque. It's not a LinkedIn post. Legacy is what remains in the soil of a place long after my name is forgotten. It's the cultural shift I ignited. It's the leader who says, "Because of him, I didn't quit." It's the truth I spoke that cracked open the next level of growth for someone who was watching. Most of all, it's the blueprint I left behind that made it easier for another Black man to lead, without having to erase himself.

What I've learned about legacy is that it isn't loud; it's layered. It lives in how people feel after working with you. It's in the language teams start using because you modeled it first. It's in the conversations people are now brave enough to have, because you went first. Legacy isn't built in performance reviews. It's built in alignment and repetition, in the daily discipline of refusing to sell yourself short just to survive another meeting.

What I want my leadership legacy to be is not that I made it. I want to be remembered as the one who redefined what "making it" looks like. I want people to say: He didn't shrink to stay safe, he stretched the room so others could fully lead. He didn't just speak truth, he modeled what it looks like to lead with it. He built systems, not just stories. People are still using his frameworks because they work. He made leadership human again.

"I used to want to be known. Now I want to be useful. If my leadership helped even one brother stand taller in a space that tried to shrink him, that's legacy."

Tariq, VP of People & Culture, National Nonprofit

I want my legacy to be a permission slip, for Black men to lead with clarity, with wholeness, with power, without having to perform for survival. That's what I'm building. That's what I'm leaving. That's what I pray echoes long after my voice is gone.

Mentorship as Multiplication

Whether it's coaching or mentorship, it's about multiplication. Too many of us have been taught to protect the seat we've earned instead of preparing space at the table. But I've learned that leadership not passed on becomes performance. Mentorship and coaching aren't just about helping out; they're about building out. It's not a program. It's not a posture. It's not just giving advice; it's creating access. And it doesn't just serve the mentee or coachee, it sharpens the mentor or coach.

I approach mentorship while building something bigger: I treat it as leadership infrastructure. I don't mentor on the side, I build it into the system. I carve out space in my schedule for intentional development. I bring emerging leaders into stretch assignments, not just into small talk. I don't hoard strategy, I share frameworks, thought processes, even mistakes. Because if you can't hand someone else the blueprint, you're not building legacy, you're just maintaining control.

I use my platform to elevate, not just to be seen. I don't just show up to shine, I show up so others can get in the room, speak in the room, and shift the room. That means passing the mic in meetings and naming who's ready, even if they're not in the official pipeline. It means being vocal about talent that looks like us but doesn't lead like the status quo. If a platform is only big enough for me, then it's not big enough.

I coach from my scars, not my résumé. I tell the truth about what challenged me, about the beliefs that almost cost me my voice, because I don't want the next generation to inherit silence wrapped in success. Mentorship isn't about creating clones; it's about uncovering clarity. I don't want them to be like me, I want them to be free to lead fully as themselves, faster and deeper than I ever could.

I build beyond my role. I'm not waiting for a title to give me permission to lead. I write. I teach. I consult. I invest in systems that won't collapse when I leave, because my leadership isn't confined to a role; it's expressed through it. What I'm building, whether books, blueprints, leaders, or movements, will outlive my position. I'm not just filling a seat; I'm creating a succession plan for freedom.

Reflection Questions:

- Who am I actively pouring into, not just passively advising?

- What system, curriculum, or culture am I creating that will stand without me?
- Am I protecting my seat, or preparing space for someone to grow beyond me?

CONCLUSION

For Black men transitioning from mid-level to senior leadership, the journey isn't just about sharpening skills, it's about reshaping identity without losing it. It's about reestablishing your leadership rhythm before the system imposes its own. The greatest threat isn't failure; it's slipping back into the patterns that once made you visible but voiceless.

My final word: you can't approach this journey casually. It demands daily commitment, because if you don't practice it with intention, the default will pull you back.

Daily Discipline: Integrating These Lessons

How I suggest integrating these lessons into your daily life is this:

First, begin every week with alignment, not just a to-do list. Ask yourself: Who do I want to be this week? Not just What do I need to produce? Also ask: Where will I need to lead from conviction, not convenience?

Second, use your values to make small decisions so you're prepared for the big ones. Whether it's how you give feedback, how you speak up in meetings, or how you create space for restoration, don't wait for a crisis to practice authenticity. Build it into your daily rhythms.

Third, reconnect with your leadership DNA regularly. Revisit the questions from Chapter Four: What's my style? What's my story? What's my standard? Keep that sheet somewhere visible. Re-anchor yourself before major decisions, and use it to filter every opportunity.

Fourth, create a check-in ritual that keeps you honest. Every Friday or Sunday, ask yourself: Did I lead from alignment or impression this week? Where did I show up fully, and where did I shrink? What do I need to recommit to?

Finally, keep people around you who will call you out, with love. You need mirrors, not hype people. You need a circle that protects your truth, not just your title. Leadership is too costly to carry in isolation.

Why does this matter? Because the system is counting on your exhaustion. It's counting on you to forget the promises you made to yourself. It's counting on your survival instincts to kick back in. But now, you've seen the map. You've done the reflection. The responsibility is yours. You don't have to hustle for belonging. You don't have to trade power for proximity. You don't have to sacrifice peace for the performance of being "ready."

Navigating Common Pitfalls

The real test begins after the transformation. If you're being honest with yourself, the hardest part isn't finding your authentic edge, it's keeping it once the applause starts. Because transformation isn't a finish line; it's a daily fight. And for Black men in leadership, that fight shows up in ways that are subtle, seductive, and dangerous if you're not paying attention.

Common pitfalls after the transformation, and how to navigate them:

First, The Approval Addiction Trap:

You begin by leading from alignment. Then the applause comes. Now they love your voice. Now you're being invited into more rooms. Suddenly, you start adjusting again, not to survive, but to be celebrated, or to stay celebrated. Navigate this by anchoring your decisions in your values, not their validation. Ask yourself: Is this true to my core, or just tailored to their comfort? Keep a circle that reminds you who you were before the applause.

Second, The Isolation Trap:

As you rise, the rooms get quieter. You become the only one, again. Fatigue creeps in. You start thinking, Nobody really gets what I'm carrying. So you retreat. You stop checking in. You lead alone. Navigate this by remembering: isolation is not strength, it's a setup. Create consistent rhythms of vulnerability with mentors, coaches, and trusted brothers in your circle. Protect that circle as fiercely as your calendar, because you'll need both.

Third, the imposter rebound trap:

You've done the internal work. You've stepped into senior spaces. But then a moment hits, a new role, a high-stakes meeting, a decision that goes sideways, and suddenly, the old voice whispers: Maybe you're not built for this. Maybe you just got lucky. Navigate this by recognizing that voice doesn't mean you're regressing, it means you're growing. Revisit your leadership DNA. Reread your wins. Name your receipts. Say out loud, "I'm not new to this; I'm aligned to this."

Fourth, the performance rebrand trap:

You've dropped the mask. You've shown up with your full voice. Now people expect a certain brand of realness, and you start performing authenticity instead of practicing it. Navigate this by remembering: authenticity doesn't mean over-disclosure, it means consistent alignment. Don't let being "real" become your new performance. Be disciplined, not performative.

Fifth, the savior syndrome trap:

You made it through. Now you feel responsible to fix everything, carry everyone, and say yes to every young brother who needs help. You burn out trying to be everything to everyone. Navigate this by remembering: you're not the answer, you're an example. Mentor, yes. Support, yes. But lead from overflow, not obligation. Create boundaries that protect your impact.

The bottom line:

Transformation is fragile unless reinforced with structure, community, and rhythm. You didn't come this far to become a new version of the same burnout cycle. You came to lead free, to stay whole, and to build what lasts. Every pitfall is an invitation back to your edge, not the loud edge, but the aligned one. The one that got you here, and the one that will carry you forward.

Reflection prompt for leaders:

Evaluate the following:

- Which pitfall is most likely to show up in my leadership right now?

- What rhythm or boundary will help me resist it before it derails me?

- Who is keeping me accountable to my authentic edge, not just my ambitions?

Maintaining Momentum and Commitment

Clarity gets you started. Discipline keeps you authentic. That moment when you finally reclaim your voice as a Black man in leadership, when you stop shape-shifting, when you speak truth into a system that never asked for it, that moment is powerful.But it's also fleeting unless you protect it. Clarity is a spark. Momentum is a rhythm. If you don't create systems around your authenticity, old habits will return, just dressed in new clothes.

Black men can stay committed to authenticity after clarity in these ways:

One: Normalize self-check-ins over self-critique. Every week, take 15 minutes to ask yourself: Where did I lead from alignment? Where did I shrink or perform? What cost me energy, and was it worth it? This isn't about guilt. It's about guardrails. Check in. Adjust. Move forward with grace and precision.

Two: Build rituals that recenter you, not just systems that exhaust you. Routines matter, but not just for productivity. You need soul systems, rituals that keep you grounded in who you are. Start your week by re-reading your leadership DNA. End your day with one question: Did I lead from who I am, or from what they expected? Block time for reflection like it's a meeting with your future self.

Three: Keep people around you who challenge you when you drift. You need folks who know your core and can say: "You sounded sharp, but that didn't sound like you." "You're back to the hustle for approval again. What's going on?" That kind of mirror is priceless. Because drift is slow, and comfort is sneaky. You need truth-tellers, not title-chasers, in your circle.

Four: Measure more than metrics. Success is easy to track. But what about peace, presence, and alignment? Create your own scoreboard: Did I rest without guilt? Did I mentor without performance? Did I say no to anything that felt out of rhythm? Authenticity needs its own analytics.

Five: Return to your why, often. Don't reclaim your edge just to stay polished. You did it to lead differently. When clarity fades, remember the cost of the mask. Remember what you promised yourself in burnout. Remember who's watching you for permission to lead. If clarity is the awakening, then discipline is the anchor.

What Sustained Transformation Looks Like

The transformation isn't a moment; it's a method. Everyone loves a breakthrough story, the day you spoke up, the moment you set a boundary, the first time you said no without apology. But real leadership transformation doesn't live in the highlight reel. It lives in the quiet, consistent decisions no one applauds.

What sustained, authentic leadership actually looks like:

It looks like protecting your rhythm, even when others expect you to grind. You still hit your goals, you still lead with strength, but now, you rest on purpose. You say no more quickly. You take Fridays off without guilt. You no longer equate overworking with worth. And if someone questions that, you don't flinch. You say, "My clarity is non-negotiable. My rhythm is part of my leadership strategy."

It looks like showing up in the room without code-switching. You don't adjust your tone to seem less threatening. You don't sit in meetings and let your brilliance be diluted for comfort. You ask bold, culture-shifting questions. You challenge respectfully and clearly, even when it's unpopular. You're not the angry one; you're the aligned one. Now, your presence shifts the room, not your posture.

It looks like choosing peace over performance, consistently. You're no longer chasing validation through visibility. You don't say yes to every panel, every mentorship request, every "Can I pick your brain?" coffee chat. You stop performing the role of the over-accessible Black leader. Now, you move with selective, strategic service, because your peace has purpose.

It looks like leading with clarity in hard decisions and difficult conversations. You don't shy away from conflict, but you also don't act impulsively. You approach tough conversations with emotional discipline and strategic truth. You don't just speak what's real, you speak what's right, because you've done the internal work. That's transformation: when your integrity shows up in the tension.

It looks like making space for others. You've stopped trying to be the only one. Now, you're inviting others in, mentoring without ego, teaching what you've learned not to impress, but to equip. You use your title as a platform, not a pedestal. You're not just leading; you're multiplying.

It looks like repeating the hard, quiet things until they become natural. You realign, reflect, and recalibrate when you drift. When you're tired, you return to the blueprint instead of defaulting to the mask. You're no longer leading from fear or ego, you're leading from alignment, daily.

The bottom line: sustained, authentic leadership transformation looks like strategy with soul, discipline without depletion, power with presence, boundaries without bitterness, and voice without volume. Here's the part no one tells you, when the transformation is real, you don't need to prove it. Your peace will speak louder than your performance ever did.

Tariq, a VP of People and Culture at a national nonprofit, once said to me: *"I didn't realize I was fully transformed until I stopped preparing for rooms that used to make me question my voice. Now I walk in knowing they're lucky I'm here."* That's what it means to fully bring yourself into a space, knowing you have no need for boundaries, because you're authentically being yourself.

A Message to the Next Generation

To the next generation of Black male leaders, here's what I need you to know: If you're reading this, and you're serious about creating a lasting impact, not just chasing quick wins and flashy titles, then I'm talking to you like a mentor who's already walked the path you're heading down. This is a long game. Lead from alignment. And never sell your soul to rent success.

Here's the truth the system won't tell you: It will praise your hustle but exploit your silence. It will applaud your performance while quietly draining your power. It will reward you for fitting in, but never truly make space for you to belong.

So, if you want to lead in a way that lasts, if you want to build something your sons, your brothers, your people can stand on, here's my advice:

First, be clear on who you are before the room tries to define you. Your voice matters. Your story matters. Your difference is your advantage, not your liability. Don't wait for permission to show up fully, and don't shape-shift just to be accepted. If you have to lose yourself to lead, that's not leadership, it's performance. Write your own script. Speak your truth. Let alignment not assimilation be your edge.

Second, build what will outlive you. Every meeting, every decision, every relationship is either feeding your ego or feeding your legacy. Choose wisely. Start now. Mentor someone. Document your process. Shape your framework. Build systems that reflect your values, not just your goals. You're not just leading for today; you're building for those you'll never meet.

Third, don't wear burnout like a badge. The system will push you to grind until you're empty, to prove you belong, to prove you're not the "angry Black man," to prove you're the safe one, the right one, the perfect fit. Forget proving. Protect your peace. Guard your rhythm. Rest with intention, because nothing great is built from exhaustion. Your wellness isn't a luxury; it's essential infrastructure for sustainable impact.

Fourth, know that power doesn't always come with a title. Some of the most transformational leadership you'll offer won't show up on an org chart. It'll show up in the young brother you pulled aside and told the truth. It'll show up in the meeting where you named the elephant in the room, with grace and courage. It'll show up in the policy you helped shift behind closed doors, and in the culture you helped protect when no one else recognized the danger. Legacy leadership is less about the spotlight and more about stewardship.

Finally, don't lead alone.

Find your people.

Find the ones who challenge your ego and protect your soul.

The ones who remind you who you are when the system tries to wear you down.

Build your circle before you need it, because you will need it. And when the pressure comes and it will you don't want to be carrying your whole calling without a community.

You don't have to lead like anyone else.

You don't have to choose between being effective and being yourself.

You don't have to trade your truth for their comfort.

Lead with strategy.

Lead with soul.

Lead like you're leaving a map, because there are Black boys watching, there are systems cracking, and there's a legacy waiting to be written with your name in the foundation.

Continuing Your Journey

The journey doesn't end here. You've finished the book. You've done the work. You've wrestled with the reflection in the mirror. You've reclaimed your voice. You've made peace with your power. But the real journey begins now, because transformation doesn't stop at the final page. Authentic leadership isn't a moment; it's a movement. It's a daily, deliberate choice.

So when you find yourself asking, What now? remember this: You are clear. You are called. But clarity without community breeds isolation. And conviction without structure often slips back into old survival patterns. That's why I didn't write this book to be the finish line. I wrote it to be your foundation. And now, I want to walk alongside you as you build what comes next, on your terms, in your rhythm, with your voice.

Here's how we continue the journey:

Join me for a leadership discovery call. You've gained the insight, now it's time to build the strategy. Whether you're navigating a high-stakes transition, leading as the only one in the room, or designing a leadership model that energizes instead of depletes you, or even if you want to bring this work into your organization, let's talk. If your company, your team, or your ERGs are ready to move beyond performative diversity optics, I'm here.

I design and facilitate custom leadership workshops for Black male leaders and their allies, those ready to build cultures rooted in safety, stretch, and legacy. My workshops cover: Leading with authenticity without assimilation; Managing burnout at senior levels; Building influence without ego and; Leading strategically and unapologetically. Let's shift the system from within.

You can also subscribe to my newsletter, Strategy + Soul: The Authentic Edge Briefing, where I share weekly leadership insights designed to challenge your grind and sharpen your alignment.

A final word from me to you:

You were never meant to perform leadership. You were built to embody it. The world doesn't need another polished professional playing the game well. It needs you, aligned, restored, sharp, and strategic.

Lead loud. Lead real. Lead in a way that outlives your role. And when you forget, when the pressure creeps in, when the room makes you question your voice again, come back to this. Come back to your edge. And if you ever need a mirror, know that I'll be here.

Legacy doesn't happen by accident. It happens when you lead like you remember who you are. So go. Build what only you can build. And let's keep building, together.

ACKNOWLEDGEMENTS

This book would not exist without the experiences, tensions, and truths that shaped me, and without the people who stood with me as I reclaimed my voice.

To every Black man who has ever felt he had to shrink to survive in leadership spaces: This is for you.

You were in my spirit with every page. Your journey, your brilliance, your quiet resilience, you are the reason this message matters. Keep leading. Keep rising. And never forget: Your authenticity is your advantage.

To my family, thank you for being my anchor. To my parents: Your prayers and persistence laid my foundation. To the elders who showed me strength without spectacle: I saw you, even when you said little.

To the next generation in my bloodline: May you never feel the need to ask for permission to be your full self in any room.

To my executive coach, Leland Thompson: You coached me into my first executive director role and offer. You believed in my vision when no one else in the room could see it. Thank you for organizing my thoughts, helping me carry the weight of leadership with integrity, and reminding me that I was already equipped.

To the leaders I've coached: You gave me a front-row seat to transformation.

You showed me that authenticity isn't just possible at the highest levels, it's powerful. Thank you for trusting me with your stories, for sharpening me, calling me out, and calling me up.

To my editor and to Mubarik H.M. Nuh: Thank you for your thoughtful editing partnership, for shaping this work with clarity, and for honoring its original spirit.

And to you, the reader, whether you found this book at a crossroads or in a moment of clarity, know this: You are not alone. You are not behind. You are not too much.

You are exactly who you need to be to lead at the highest level, without losing yourself.

Thank you for walking this journey with me. Now, let's build legacy.

Dominic George

Author | Coach | Founder, Vision Leadership for LIFE

ABOUT THE AUTHOR

Dominic George is a leadership strategist, speaker, and executive coach who equips Black men to rise in leadership without losing themselves in the process.

As the Founder of Vision Leadership for LIFE, Dominic has guided hundreds of mid-level and senior leaders across corporate, nonprofit, government, tech and education sectors, helping them navigate power, politics, and pressure with clarity, strategy, and soul.

A former executive with deep experience in high-stakes organizational leadership, Dominic knows firsthand what it means to lead while Black, succeed while under surveillance, and deliver results without a roadmap. His work centers the realities of high-achieving Black men who are often the only ones in the room, and gives them the tools to lead unapologetically and sustainably.

Dominic is the creator of The Authentic Performance™ Model, a framework designed to help leaders align purpose with measurable outcomes, reclaim their voice, and build high-performing cultures without code-switching or burnout.

Rooted in lived experience and sharpened by years of coaching, Dominic's message is clear:

You don't have to conform to lead. You have to remember who you are.

Through one-on-one coaching, organizational workshops, and his work building the Vision Leadership Academy, Dominic is committed to growing the next generation of legacy-driven Black male leaders, those who lead with alignment, not assimilation.

When he's not coaching or speaking, Dominic can be found mentoring emerging leaders, developing curriculum for culturally relevant leadership development, or recharging with family and faith.

Connect with Dominic at VisionLeadershipForLife.com or follow his journey at www.linkedin.com/in/dominiccgeorge on LinkedIn.

www.ingramcontent.com/pod-product-compliance
Lightning Source LLC
Chambersburg PA
CBHW072006090426
42740CB00011B/2108